Eugene Rousseau
SAXOPHONE HIGH TONES

A Systematic Approach to the Extension of the Range of All the Saxophones: Soprano, Alto, Tenor and Baritone

Second Edition

A Division of
LAUREN KEISER MUSIC PUBLISHING

Saxophone High Tones
Second Edition

Eugene Rousseau

Copyright © 1978, 2002 Norruth Music, Inc. Copyright assigned 2008 to Lauren Keiser Music Publishing (ASCAP). All rights reserved. International Copyright Secured. No part of this publication may be reproduced, stored in a retrieval system, or transmitted—in any form or by any means now known or later developed—without prior written permission from the publisher except in the case of brief quotations embodied in critical articles and reviews.

ISBN: 1-58106-005-X
Printed in USA

For information and catalogs, contact:

Keiser Productions, Inc.

Phone: 203-560-9436
Fax: 314-270-5305
Email: info@keiserproductions.com
Website: keiserproductions.com

TABLE OF CONTENTS

PREFACE TO THE FIRST EDITION iv
PREFACE TO THE SECOND EDITION iv
FOREWORD v
FINGERING CHART FOR THE NORMAL RANGE vi

GETTING STARTED 1

    The Embouchure 1
    The Harmonic Series 1
    Closed Tube Exercises 2
    Acoustics and Venting 7
    Vent Key Exercises 12
    Overblowing Sixths 14
    Venting with RSK4 15
    The Modes of Overtones 22
    Bridging the Registers 26
    Combining Modes for Practical Solutions 31
    Beyond the Sixths 34

FINGERING CHART FOR THE HIGH TONES 37

    Soprano 37
    Alto 39
    Tenor 41
    Baritone 43

HIGH TONE EXERCISES 47

    Chromatic Patterns 47
    Major Scales: One Octave 51
    Major Scales: Extended Range 52
    Major Arpeggios 56
    Minor Scales, Harmonic: One Octave 57
    Minor Scales, Harmonic: Extended Range 58
    Minor Arpeggios 63
    Minor Scales, Melodic: One Octave 64
    Minor Scales, Melodic: Extended Range 65
    Whole-tone Scales 69
    Augmented Arpeggios 70
    Diminished (Octatonic) Scales 71
    Diminished Arpeggios 73
    Patterns in Thirds 75
    Pentatonic Scales 76

ARTICULATING THE HIGH TONES 79

PREFACE TO THE FIRST EDITION

The possibilities for differences in the kinds of expression utilized in playing the saxophone are perhaps as varied as the range of capabilities exhibited by the instrument's countless performers. That the saxophone, this youthful member of the wind family, is already well established as an instrument of enormous potential goes almost without saying. The list of esteemed saxophonists throughout the world, encompassing all manner of musical styles and tastes, is immense, and growing steadily. Musical literature for the instrument includes original and transcribed works from virtually every era of musical history, with the contemporary composers—happily, to an increasing degree—continually discovering its abundant resources.

Among the many facets of the saxophone's evolution is the one to which the present book addresses itself, namely harmonics or overtones—those high tones above the normal range. A keen and widespread interest has for many years been exhibited by players, teachers, and composers in the extension of the saxophone's range upward, beyond the normal one. Indeed, the author himself shares in this interest, which has been the mainspring for the pages that follow.

Eugene Rousseau
April, 1978

PREFACE TO THE SECOND EDITION

Since its first appearance more than two decades ago, *Saxophone High Tones* has become a reference work for many saxophonists. Beyond that, however, it has continued to be a subject to which the author has given much time and reflection in encountering many students of the instrument, not the least of whom is the author himself. The teaching-learning process is ongoing and, as Marcel Mule often told his students, *"On n'arrive jamais."* (One never arrives.)

As might be expected, this second edition includes many more fingerings. More important, however, is the classification of fingerings, their derivations, characteristics, and implementation. The expression, "If you can play one saxophone you can play them all" was some years ago accepted as common wisdom. Increasingly, teachers and players are learning that this is simply not true. Therefore, although the alto is played and studied more than the other members of the saxophone family, attention is given in this volume to the differences among the soprano, tenor, and baritone.

The ability to exhibit fluency in playing above the saxophone's normal range is no longer a frill, nor is it an option; it is a necessity. The journey of learning is a continuum, without, as Maître Mule has said, an arrival point. It is the sincere hope of the author that these pages will help in making the high tones journey an illuminating one.

Eugene Rousseau
September, 2000
Minneapolis

FOREWORD

Since the publication of its first edition in 1978, I have often referred to Eugene Rousseau's valuable work, *Saxophone High Tones.* It is an indispensable pedagogical tool for students at the Paris Conservatory. I find in *Saxophone High Tones* a successful synthesis of the study of natural harmonics (overblowing), and the study of special fingerings, which allows the player to adapt to all sorts of playing situations. Moreover, the series of range exercises offers a practical means of putting these newly acquired skills into practice.

With the results of still more research on the acoustical aspects of the extended register, as well as numerous additional proposed fingerings, this second edition gives me everything I could wish for. I extend my warmest thanks to Eugene Rousseau for this brilliant contribution to the teaching of the saxophone.

Claude Delangle
Professor of Saxophone
Paris Conservatory

FINGERING CHART FOR THE NORMAL RANGE

Left Thumb

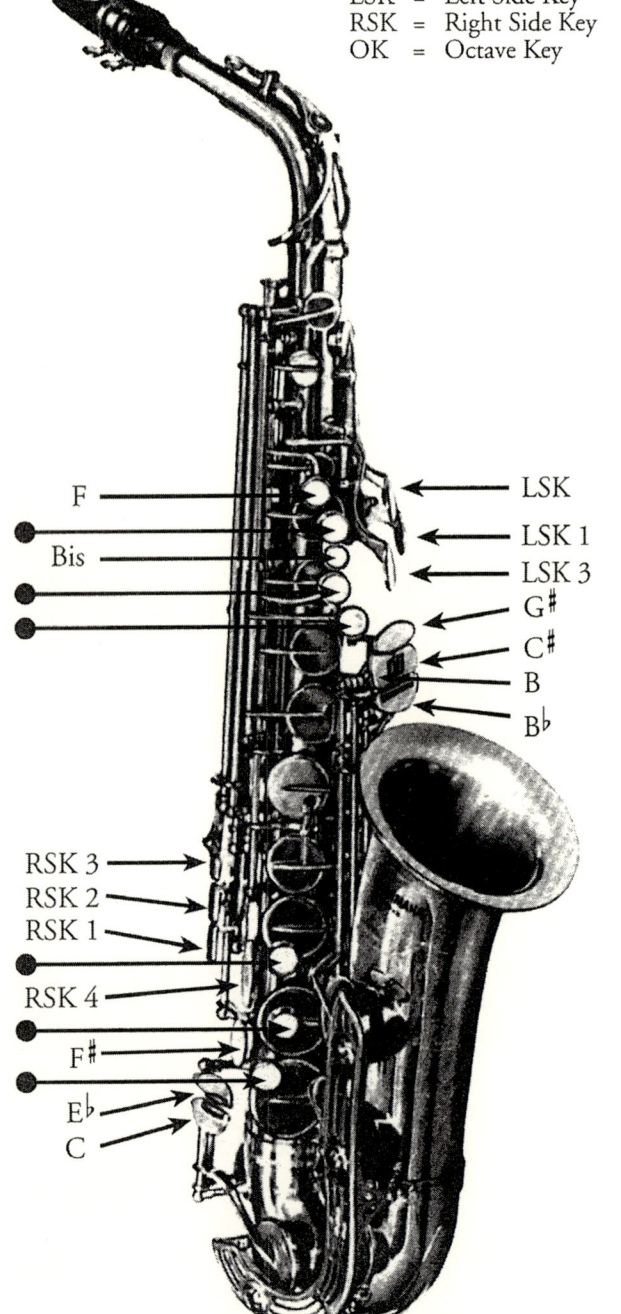

LSK = Left Side Key
RSK = Right Side Key
OK = Octave Key

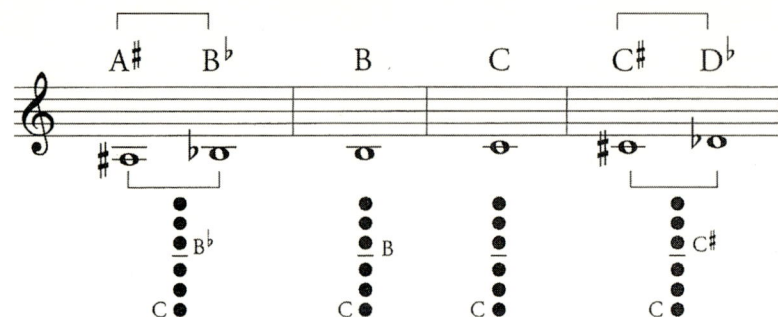

Fingerings shown are for lower notes.
For upper notes add octave key.

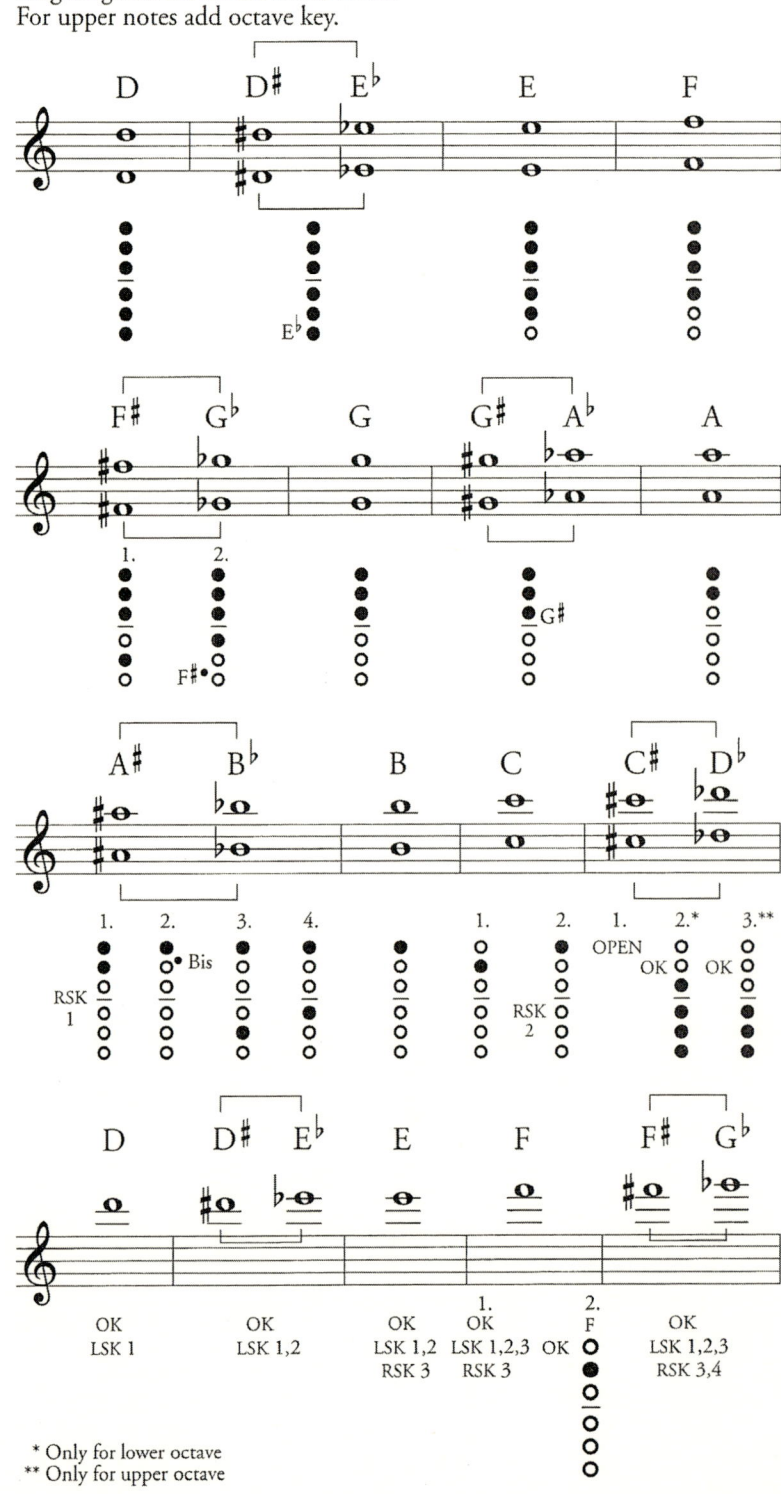

* Only for lower octave
** Only for upper octave

vi

GETTING STARTED

The Embouchure

The requisite for accomplishing harmonics or overtones on the saxophone is a good tone. In turn, the accomplishment of a good tone on the saxophone, as on all wind instruments, depends upon a proper embouchure.

While the scope of this book does not include those elements of playing normally associated with beginners, it is nonetheless essential that one have a thorough understanding of the fundamentals of the saxophone embouchure before attempting to achieve any high tones above the normal range of the instrument. These fundamentals are as follows:

1. Curl lower lip slightly over teeth.
2. Keep chin in a natural position.
3. Form an "oo" shape (as in saying coo) with the mouth and lips.
4. Form a circular shape with the mouth (the lower lip should appear somewhat bunched).
5. Place mouthpiece alone in the mouth with top teeth resting solidly on the top of the mouthpiece.
6. The round "oo" shape should now give solid support all around the mouthpiece.

The Test to determine the proper amount of mouthpiece needed in the mouth as well as the strength of the roundness and bite is to blow on the mouthpiece alone to attain the *concert pitch* shown below. Always play this test at *fortissimo* level.

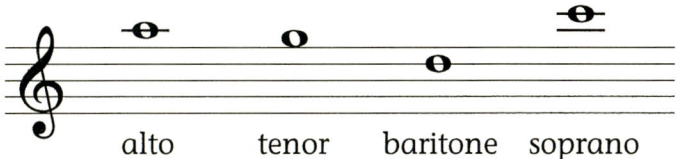

If the pitch produced on the mouthpiece alone is higher than indicated in the staff above, direct the air stream down, remembering always to keep the embouchure solid. If the pitch on the mouthpiece alone is too low, direct the air stream up. In either case never loosen the embouchure, which should remain solid at all times, while the air does its job properly.

The Harmonic Series

Each tone produced on a wind instrument is comprised of several tones, a phenomenon known as the harmonic series. Although not heard as the principal tone, some harmonics are present in varying degrees of strength when the principal tone is sounded. The main tone, or fundamental tone, is the strongest of these several tones and is the pitch that is heard. Each of the other tones is called a harmonic, or overtone—terms quite familiar to any saxophonist interested in high tones above the normal range.

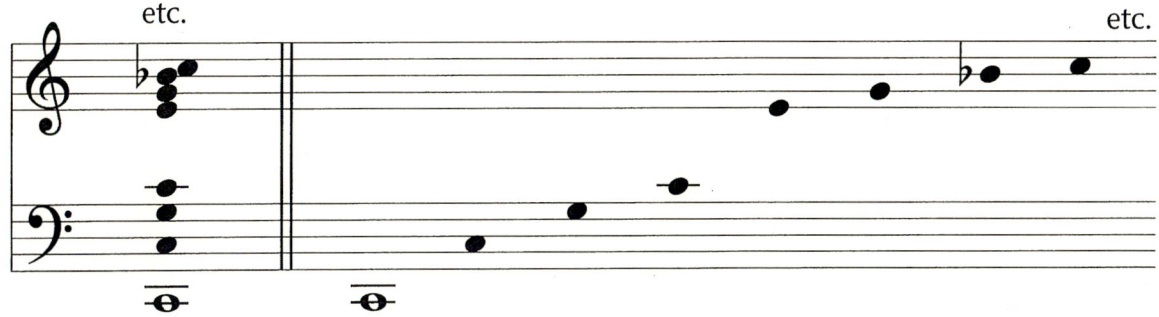

By changing the embouchure and air pressure it is possible to bypass the fundamental, thereby causing one of the harmonics to be heard as the main pitch. For this purpose the saxophone embouchure needs to be stronger than normal (a stronger circle), with *slightly* more reed exposed within the mouth. This should be realized by a very slight forward movement of the jaw rather than taking more mouthpiece into the mouth.

The air pressure must be increased as the higher harmonics are attempted—the effect being a smaller quantity of air put to use. This technique will equate with a higher pitch on the mouthpiece alone, following the testing procedure described on page 7.

The following series of tones, the harmonic series, may be practiced on all the saxophones in the manner indicated. It will be evident that (1) the harmonics work less well as one ascends to the higher fundamentals—B, C, C♯, etc.— and (2) the closed tube harmonics are more difficult on the soprano, owing to its short tube.

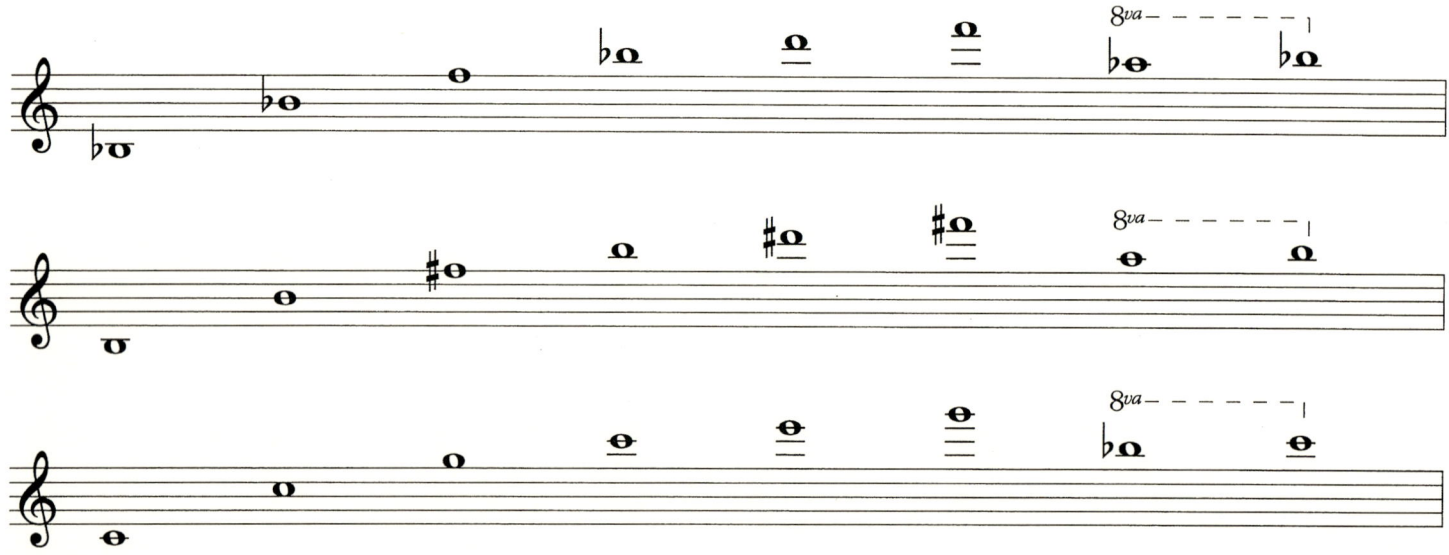

Closed Tube Exercises

Acoustics and Venting

In acoustical terms a vibrating air column produces a tone on a wind instrument, although this column of air does not vibrate uniformly throughout its length. The point at which it vibrates most vigorously is called an *anti-node*, while the point of minimum air notion is called a *node*.

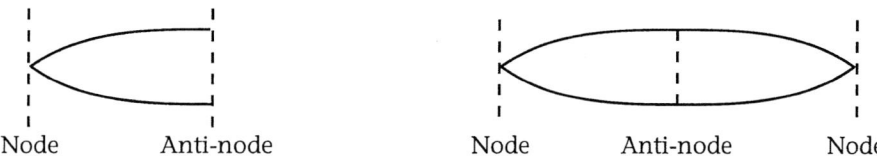

When a wind instrument sounds its fundamental tone, also known as the *first mode of vibration*, the length of tubing involved is made up of one unit that contains one *node* and one *anti-node*. Two *nodes* and two *anti-nodes* are required to produce a tone one octave higher.

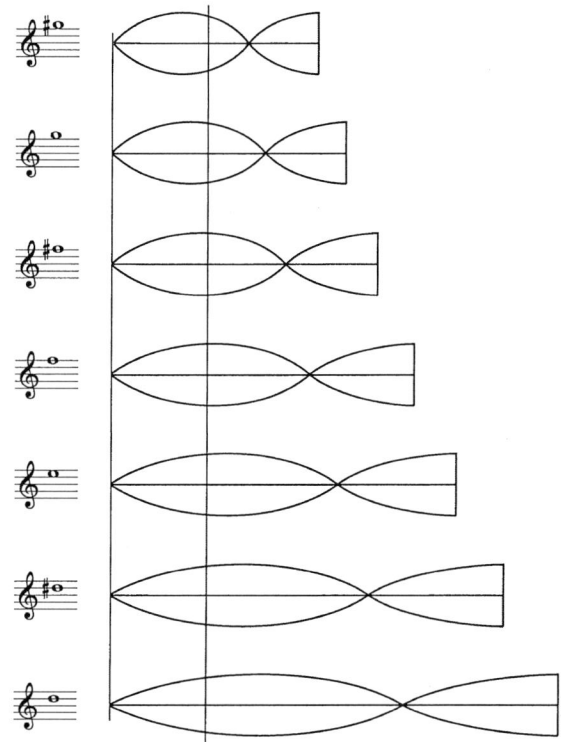

Position of lower octave key in relation to anti-nodes of each tone. Ideally the octave position should coincide with the anti-node.

The examples below indicate the approximate position of the saxophone's two octave holes. Ideally, the octave hole position should coincide with the anti-node, an arrangement that would demand an extensive series of octave holes, a highly impractical proposition. Thus, a number of compromises become necessary in building a saxophone.

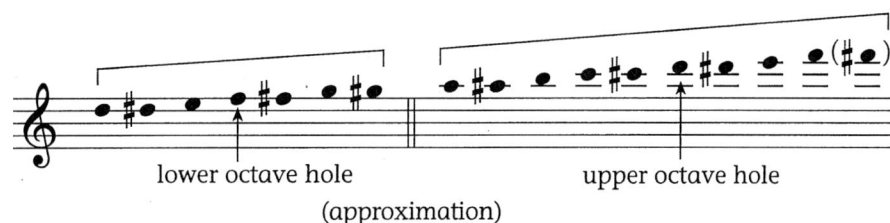

As discussed earlier, it is not only possible but often highly desirable to derive more than one tone from the same basic fingering. Many times the small, yet vitally necessary adjustment is simply the opening of a key. This slight opening, when employed to produce overtones, may be referred to as a *vent* and the process itself as *venting*. Almost all saxophones possess two *vent tubes* commonly called *octave keys*.

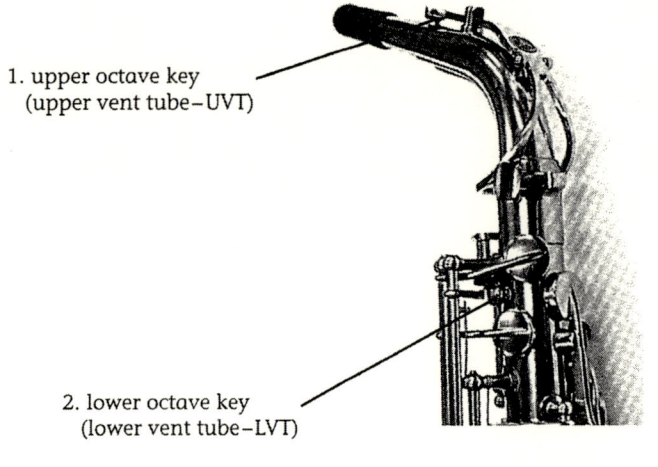

1. upper octave key (upper vent tube–UVT)
2. lower octave key (lower vent tube–LVT)
3. fundamental tones
4. octaves produced with lower octave key (LVT)
5. octaves produced with upper octave key (UVT)

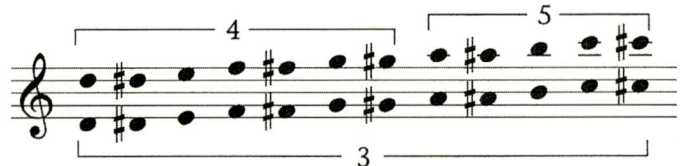

The most common example of venting, other than the use of the octave keys, occurs with key F*, sometimes designated the F auxiliary key, or front F key.

This key is usually used in conjunction with the fingering for 🎵 and most commonly used for the interval 🎵. The 🎵 thus produced does not result as an overtone of 🎵, however, but rather of 🎵. Therefore 🎵 is derived from 🎵 by using the F key as a vent.

On most saxophones the F key opens to a distance greater than necessary. This can be demonstrated by one person playing 🎵 while a second person opens LSK 3, the equivalent of the normal front F opening. Continuing to play, LSK 3 is lowered until barely open. While the quality of 🎵 may change to some degree, it nonetheless continues to sound. This technique will be refined and used extensively in the pages that follow.

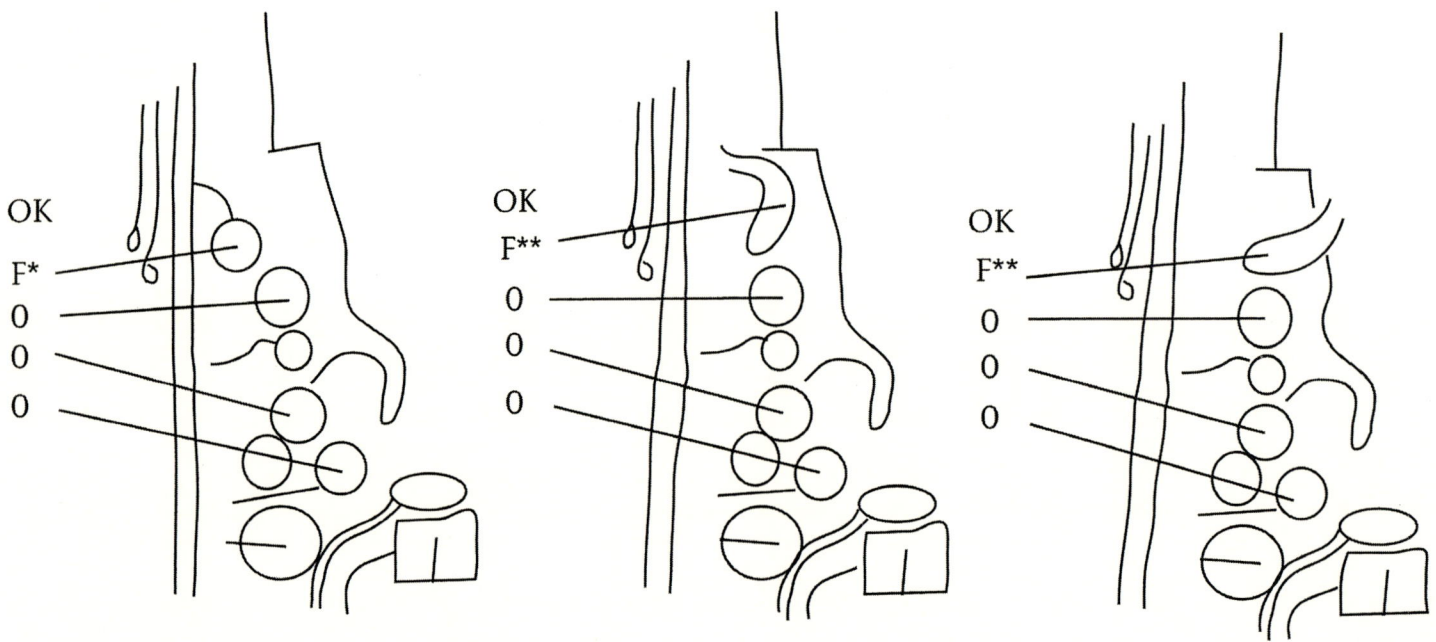

*Fingerings and key designations are on page vi.
**Virtually all current professional model saxophones have key F shaped as a spatula enabling this key to be pressed while keeping the index finger on the first main key of the left hand.

As LSK 3 assumes the true function of a vent key, a conflict between it and the lower octave key (LVT) is created. As a consequence, a successful approach to the use of LSK 3 as a vent tube is most often made by eliminating entirely the use of the upper octave key. At this point the performer should use a small flat object (paper, old reed, etc.) of approximately 0.25mm thickness (ca. 1/100 inch) to hold LSK 3 open. With LSK 3 open in this manner, and with the octave key not being used, the following series may be played on alto or tenor.

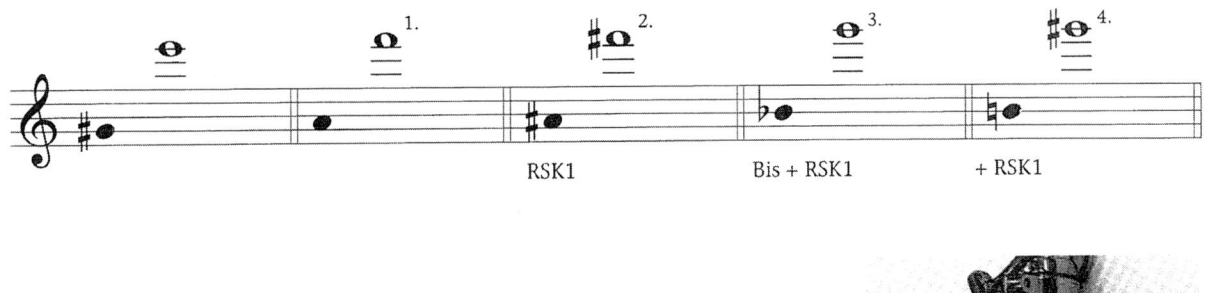

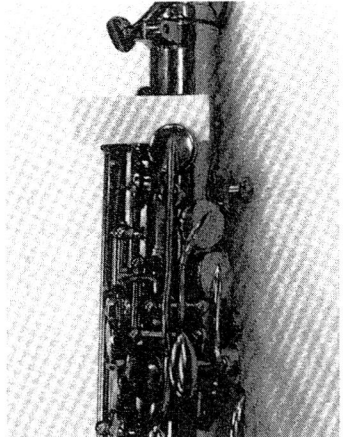

● = note fingered, and with LSK3 open ca. 0.25 mm.
○ = note to be produced
(Begin each tone without tonguing)

[1] flat on most tenors
[2] extremely flat on most tenors; not useable
[3] usually the equivalent of F# on tenor
[4] usually the equivalent of G on tenor

While the above is almost always the easiest way to begin these high tones, the same approach with the octave key should also be practiced, as this will be nearer to actual performance conditions.

Remember that both of the above examples are designed to be an aid in the development of a facility for the high tones. As these exercises are mastered, one series of fingerings normally used in performance is:

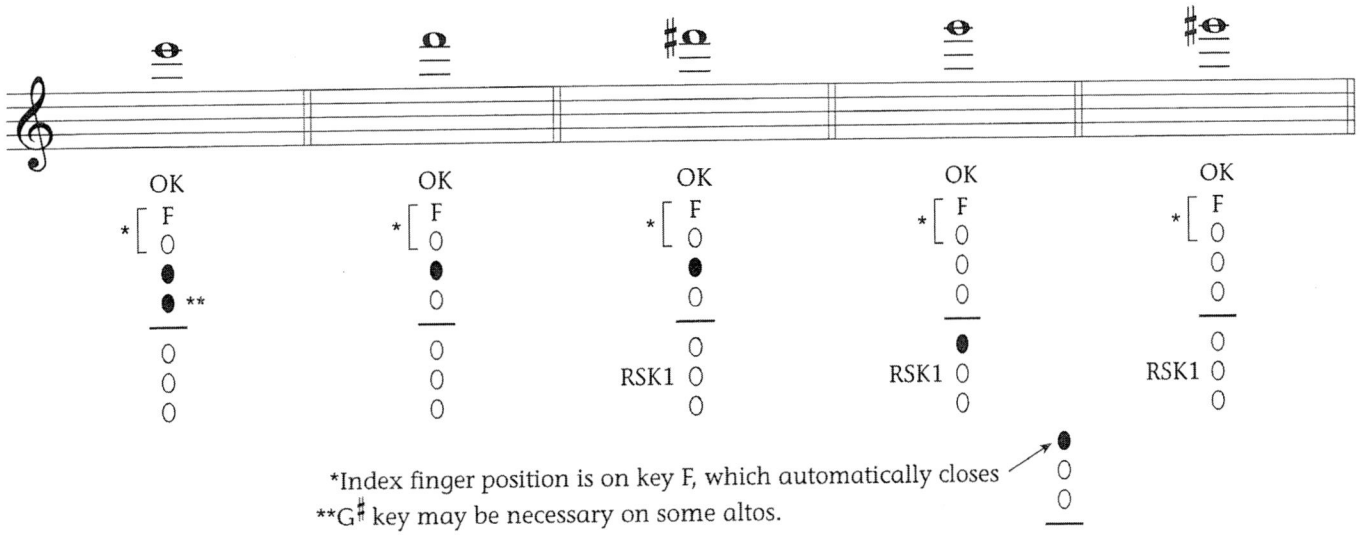

*Index finger position is on key F, which automatically closes
**G# key may be necessary on some altos.

One possible set of fingerings for the tenor:

Today's professional model saxophones (*e.g.,* Selmer SuperAction, Yamaha Custom) have adjustment screws for regulating the opening of key F. For earlier instruments (*e.g.,* Selmer Mark VI, Yamaha 62) it is possible to adjust key F so that its opening is decreased, enhancing its function as a vent key, without causing any adverse effect. Indeed, many of the author's pupils have made this adjustment themselves with highly favorable results (see photos).

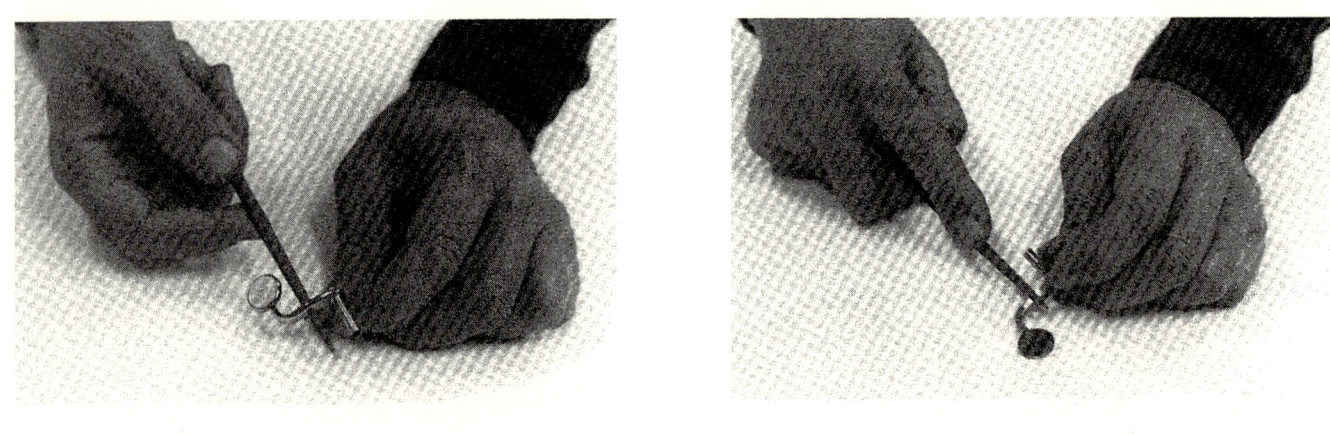

Soprano Saxophone:

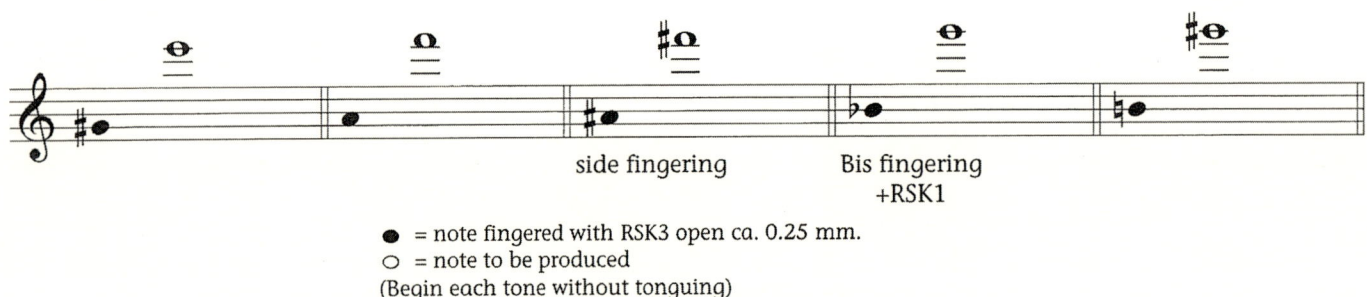

● = note fingered with RSK3 open ca. 0.25 mm.
○ = note to be produced
(Begin each tone without tonguing)

As with the alto and tenor, the same series *with* the octave key should also be practiced.

10

Digital and photographic copying of this page is illegal.

One set of fingerings for soprano:

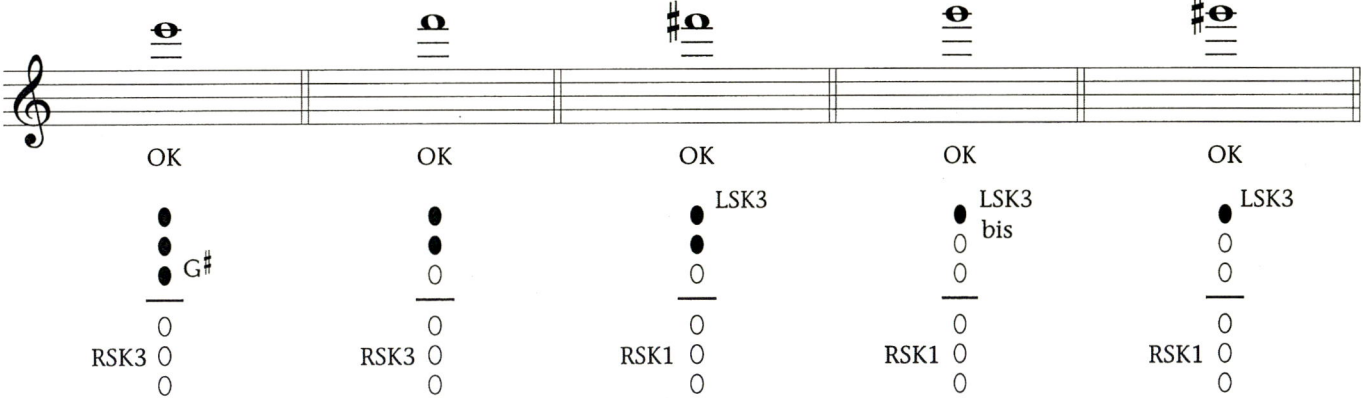

Another set if your soprano has key F:

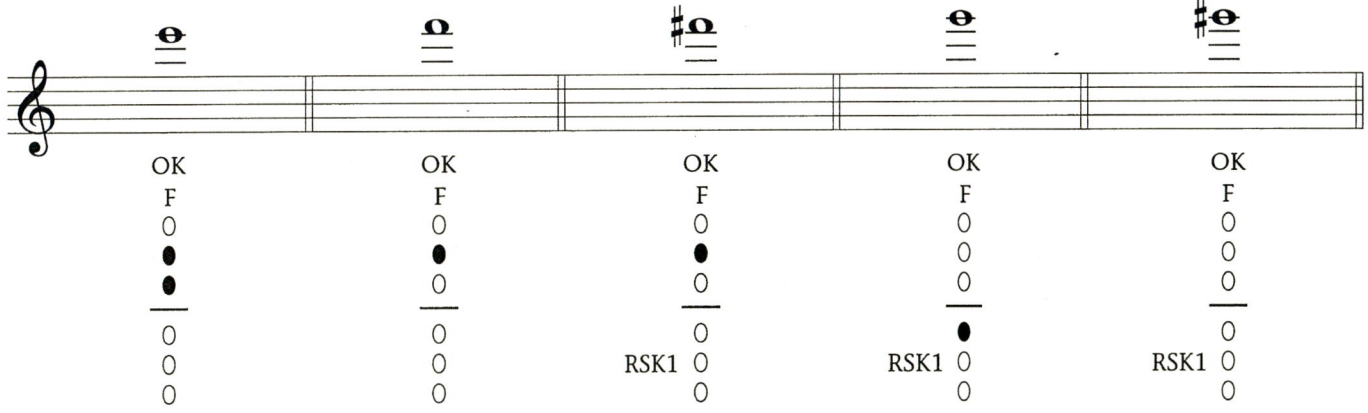

For the baritone the overblowing is:

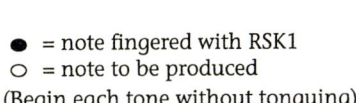

● = note fingered with RSK1
○ = note to be produced
(Begin each tone without tonguing)

Baritone fingerings that may be used in performance:

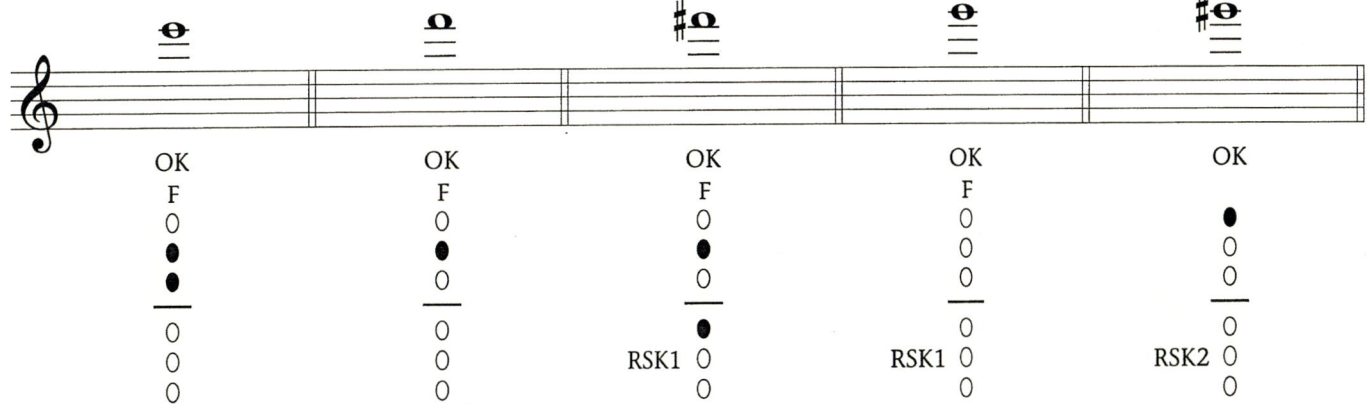

Vent Key Exercises

Practice 1–6 without tonguing

sempre *f*

Overblowing Sixths

While the natural overtone series is produced when using the closed tube, the overtone series becomes distorted as the tube is made shorter. This is most evident when using key F to overblow a sixth higher. Key F acts as a vent, allowing the next overtone to be produced quite easily. In this series, the normal overtones would be an octave, then a fifth higher than that octave. In this case, however, the second overtone is a minor sixth. An understanding of these aberrations in the normal overtone pattern is useful in developing one's skill in playing high tones. The deviation continues as a shorter amount of the saxophones's tube is used.

The necessity and practicality of venting having been discussed, it is now appropriate to outline the technique of overblowing sixths. The nature of the saxophone's tube being conical lends itself to a relatively easy production of sixths beginning with ♯♩ and continuing chromatically to ♩(♯♩) ; the result being the production of ♪♩ ♩ ♯♩ ♩(♯♩) or ♩♪♩ ♩ ♯♩ ♩(♩) in the case of the baritone.

The great value of this technique is three-fold:
1. as an aid for the development of a facility in playing high tones;
2. as a marvelous way in which to develop embouchure and air control;
3. as an enormous help in enhancing the saxophone tones in the range ♩–♯♩ .

The initial attempts at overblowing sixths may prove unsuccessful, although the method is easier than one might first imagine. The following guidelines will be helpful:
1. Begin with ♭♩ ♩ or ♩ ♯♩ which for many players are often the easiest combinations.
2. More mouthpiece inside the mouth will aid in producing the sixths—but it is a crutch that must not be used in playing music.
3. Do not tongue any tones in these exercises, since the tongue—for the very purpose of achieving the high tones—is not in its normal position for tonguing.

This is not to suggest that the high tones cannot be articulated. Tonguing in the above-normal range, however, is a complex matter and is treated separately (see p. 79).

The soprano, alto, and tenor saxophones will overblow at a major sixth while the baritone overblows at a minor sixth. Generally, the harmonics are easiest to produce on the largest saxophone, and conversely most difficult to produce on the smallest one. Thus, the soprano player will, with rare exceptions, experience the greatest challenge among saxophonists attempting to extend the range.

Soprano, Alto, and Tenor:

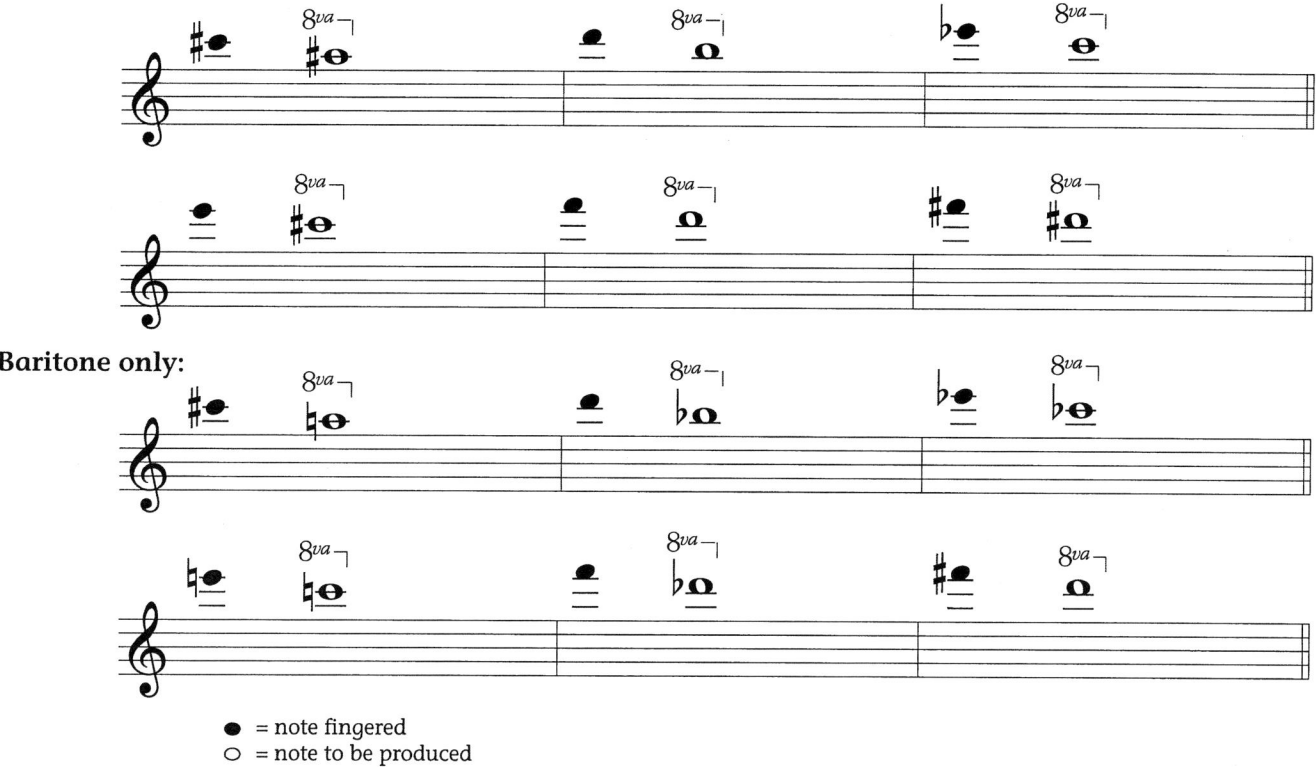

Baritone only:

● = note fingered
○ = note to be produced

Venting with RSK4

RSK4 is also very useful in producing some notes a sixth higher.

+ RSK4   + RSK4   + RSK4

The three notes above are sharp when played with these fingerings. They can be played in tune, however, and the advantages they afford are well worth the effort.

Some examples:

Soprano, Alto, Tenor:

Baritone:

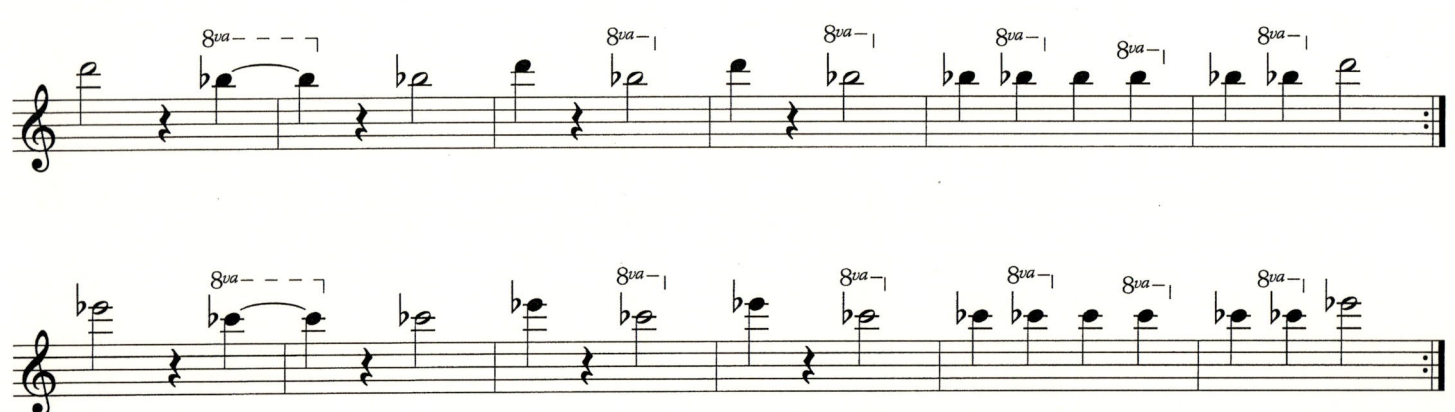

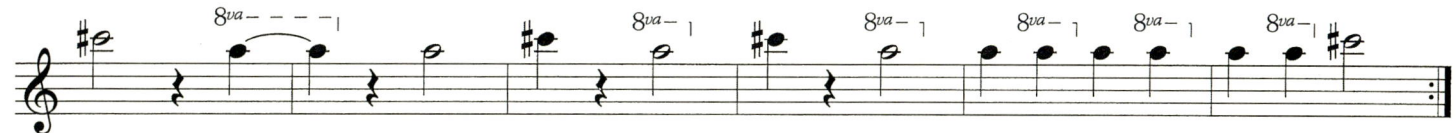

All Saxophones:

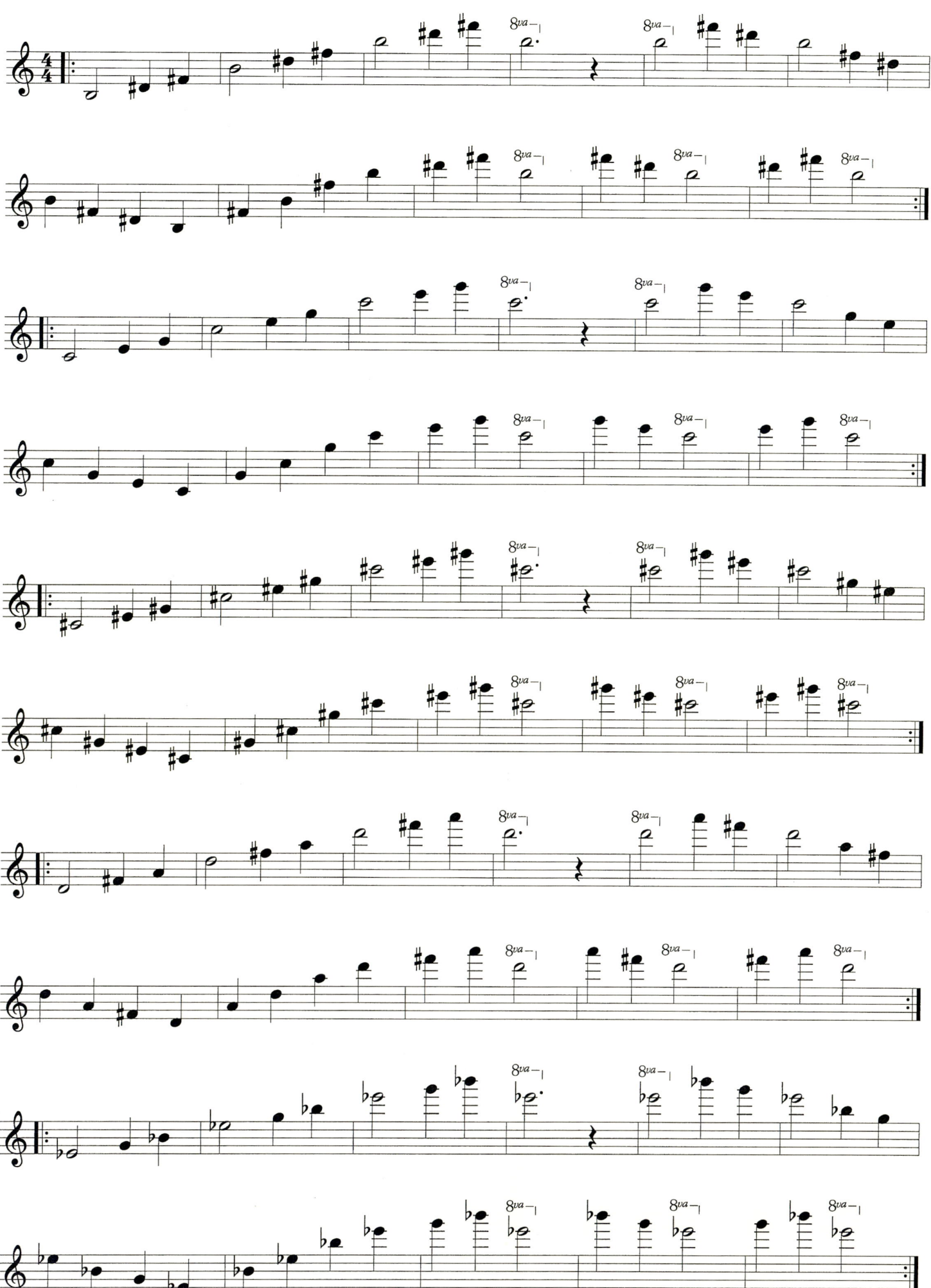

Soprano, Alto, Tenor:

Slowly

Baritone:

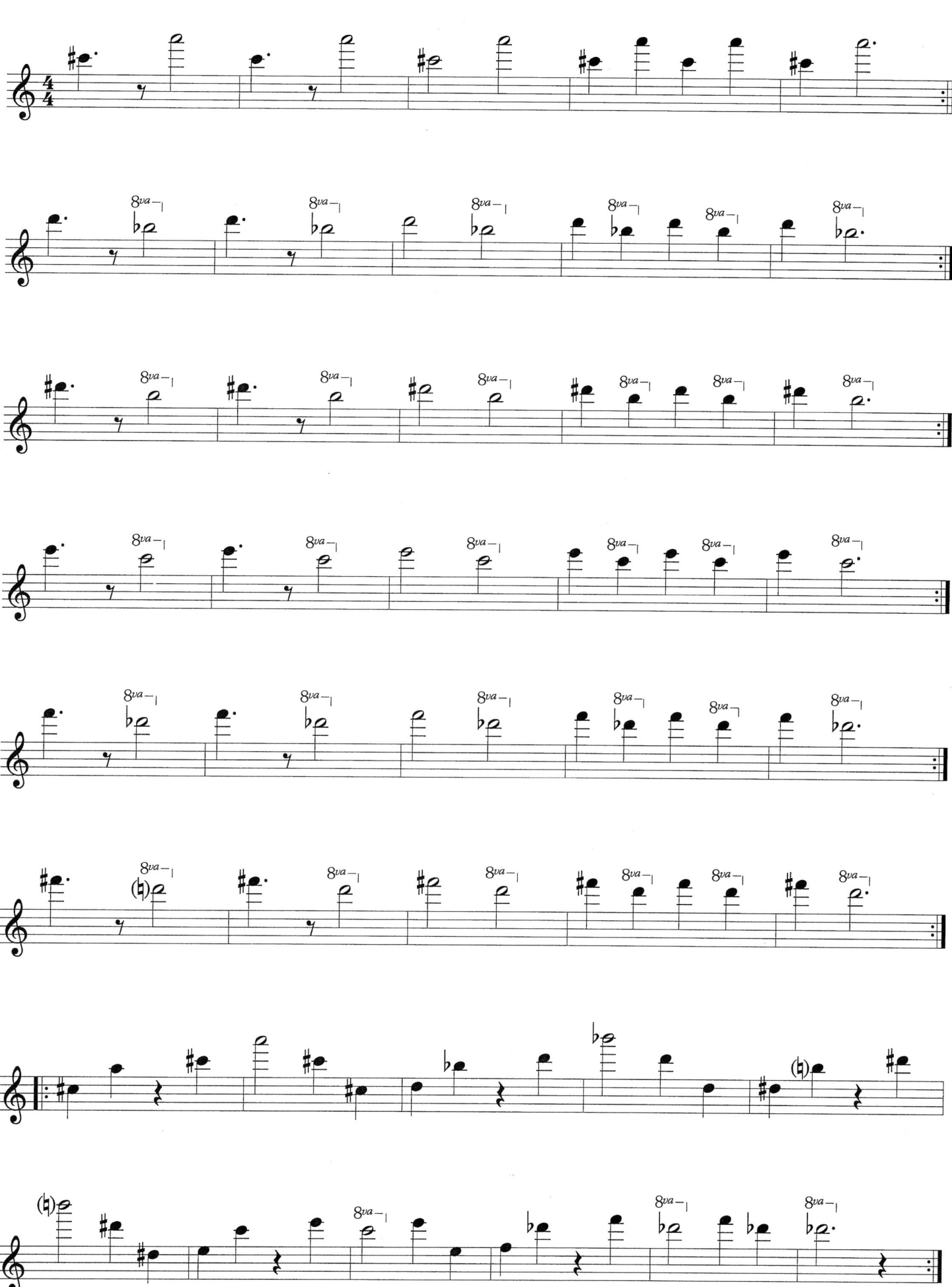

The Modes of Overtones

Since each overtone is derived from a fundamental tone, fingerings for any note above the normal range of the saxophone are related to that fundamental. There are many different timbral and response characteristics produced by the various fingerings. Below are examples of fingerings for each saxophone that employ differing modes.

Soprano:

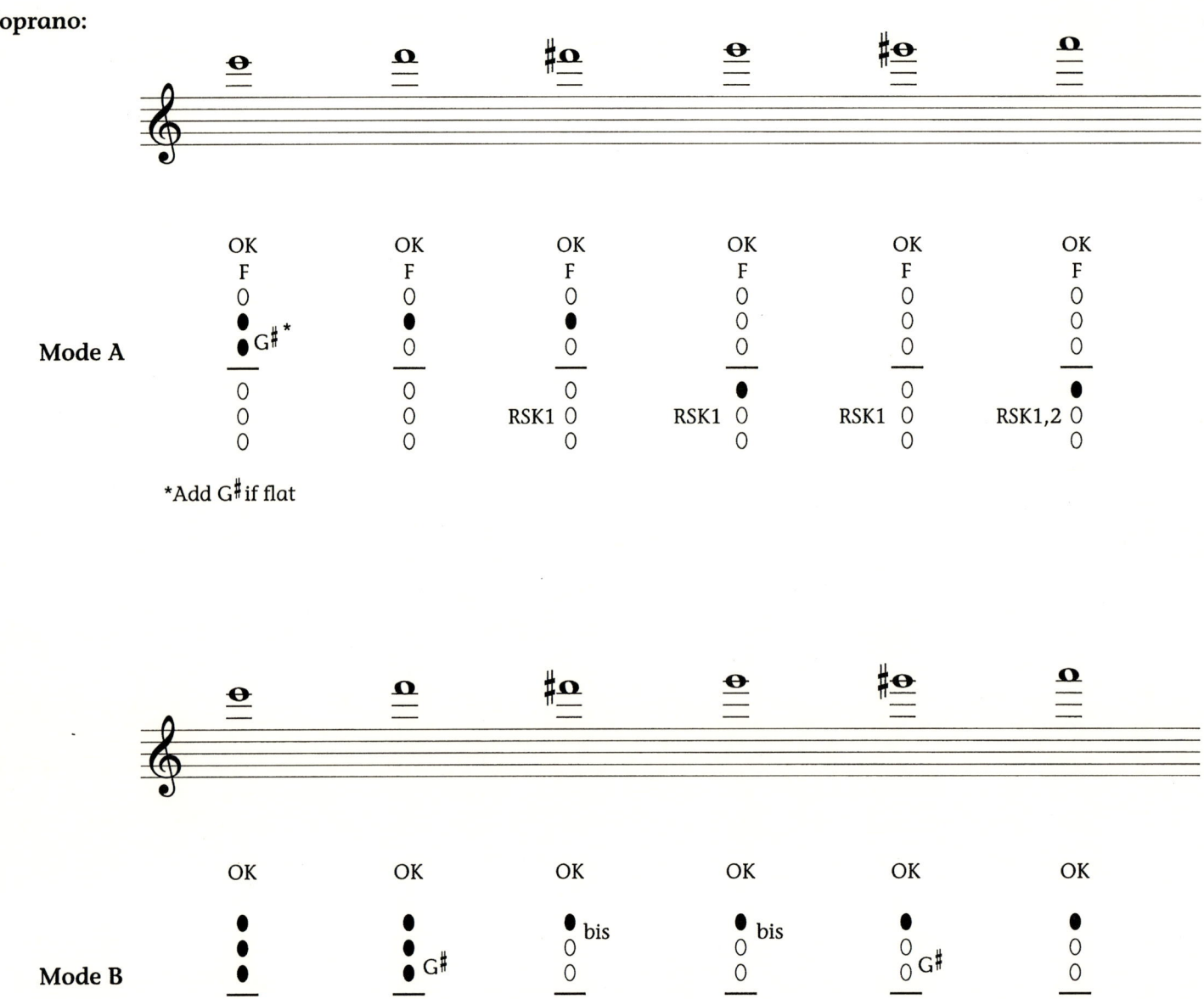

Alto:

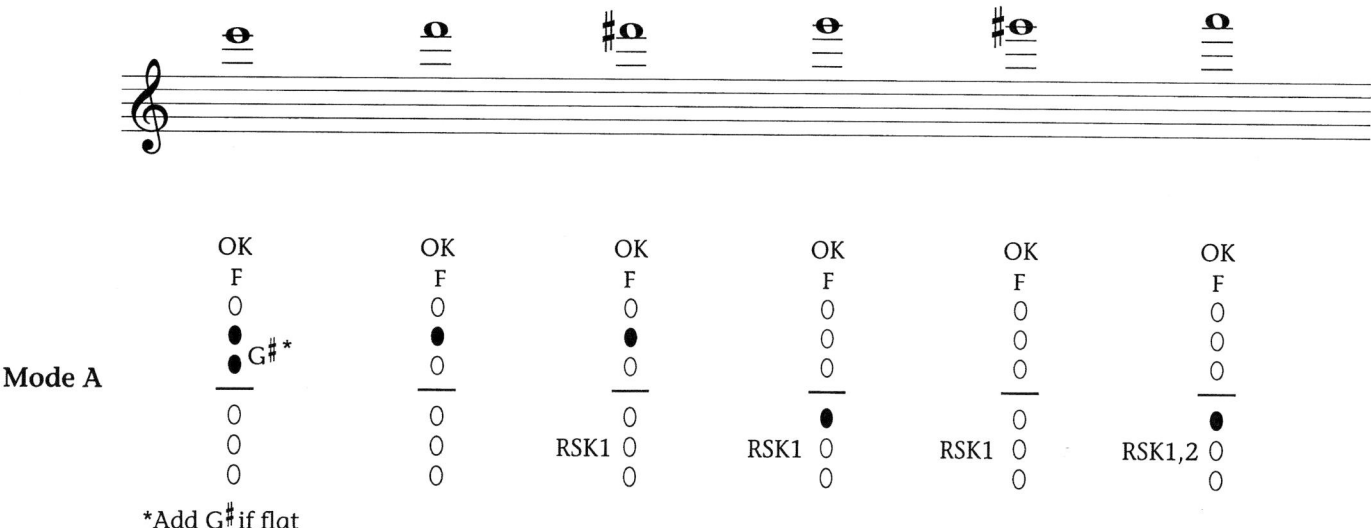

Mode A

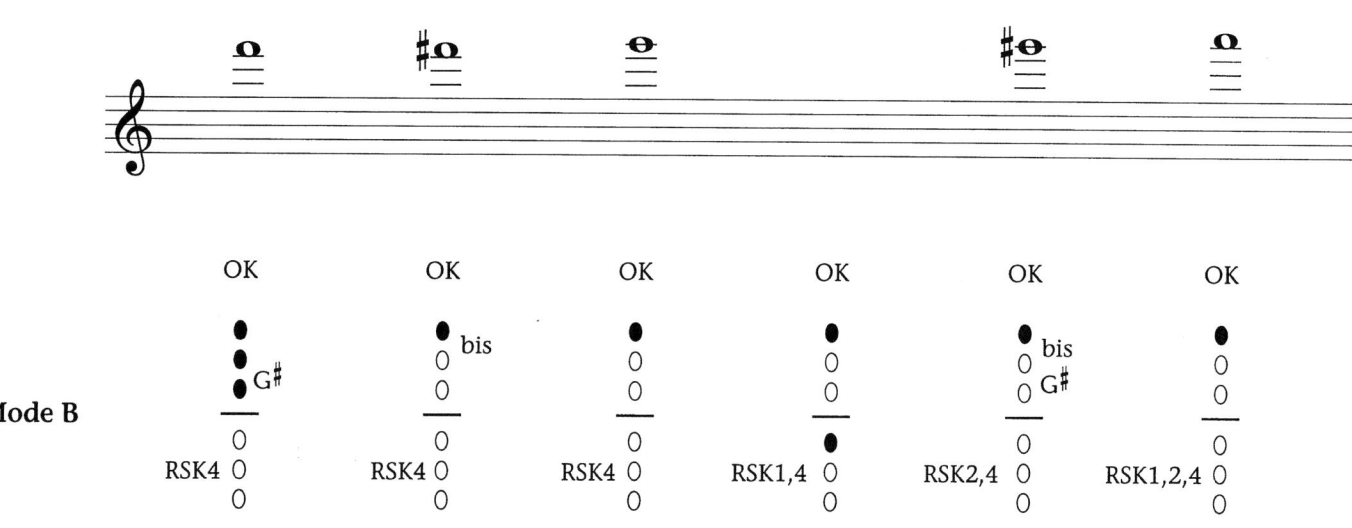

Mode B

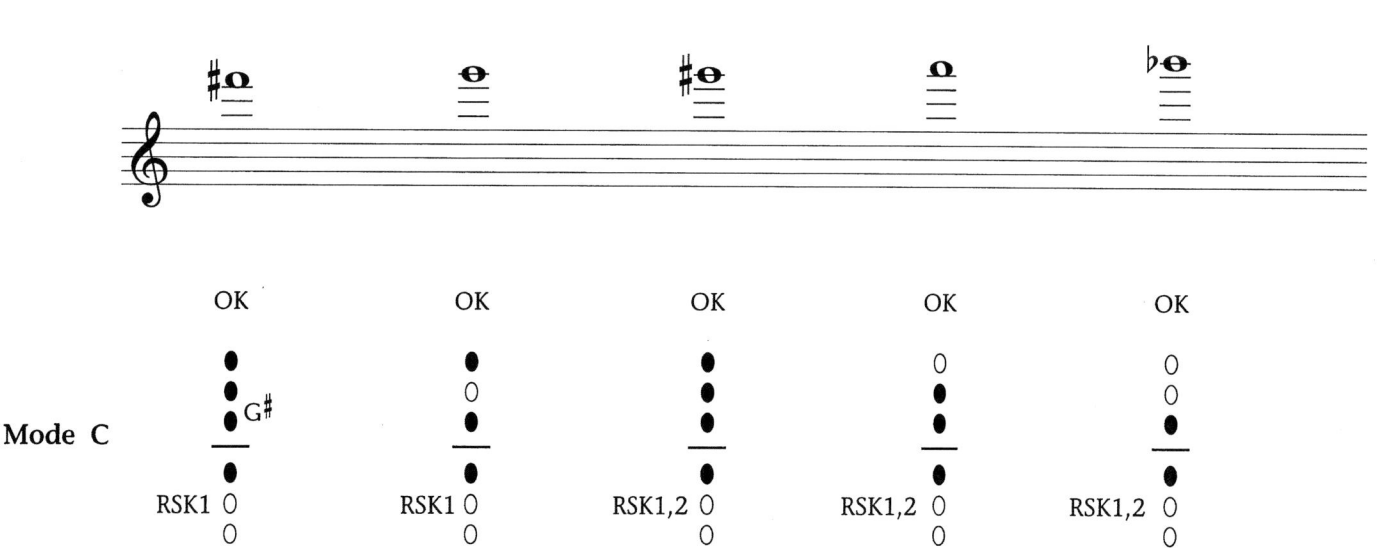

Mode C

Tenor:

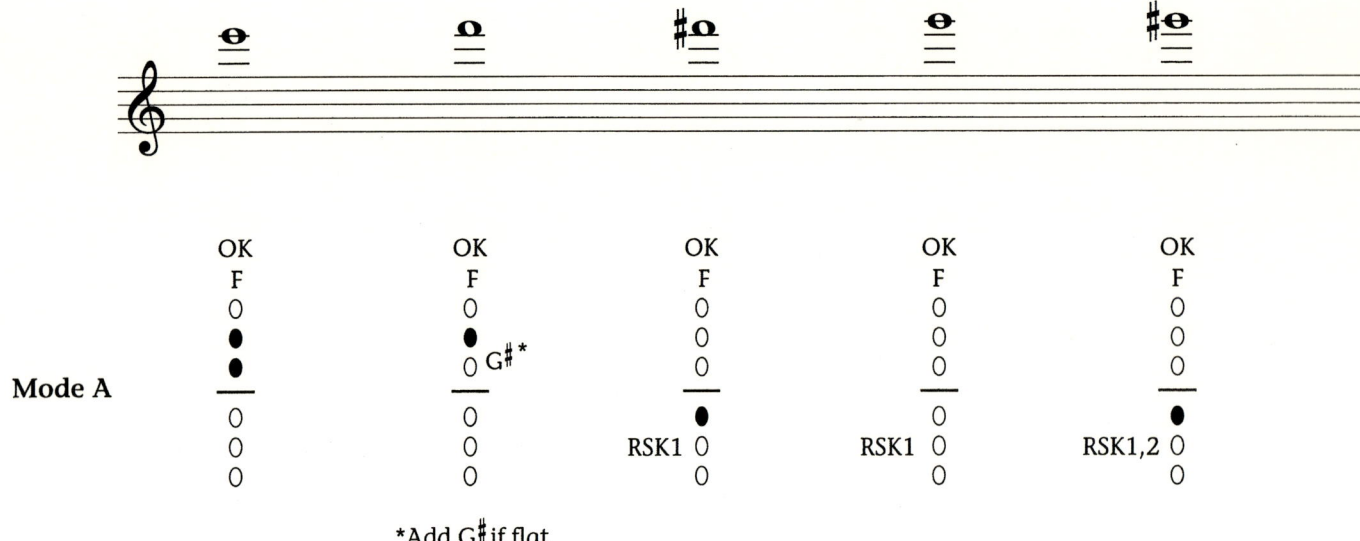

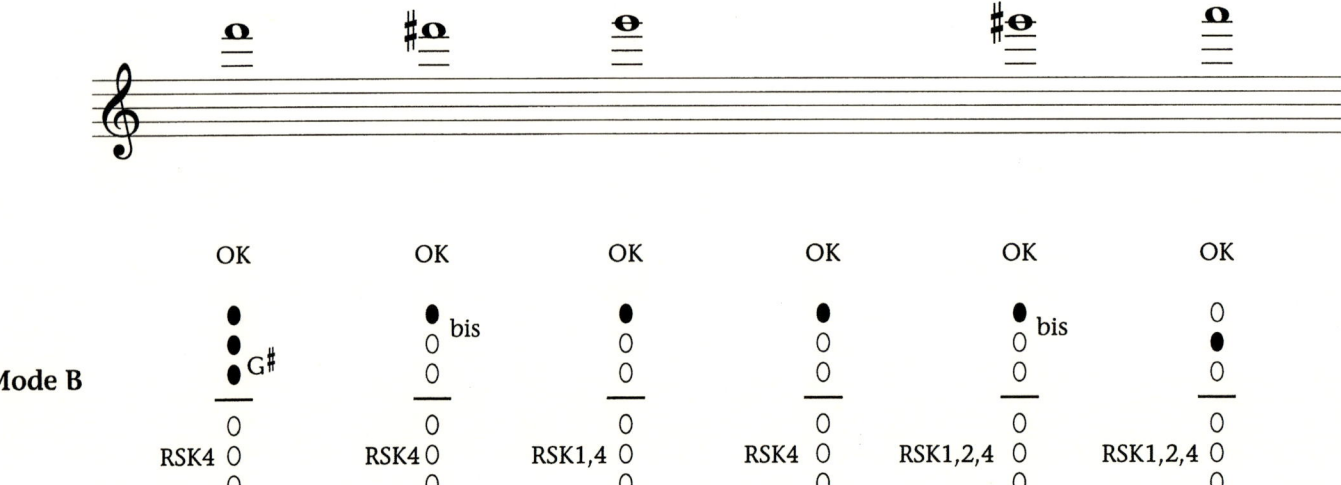

Baritone:

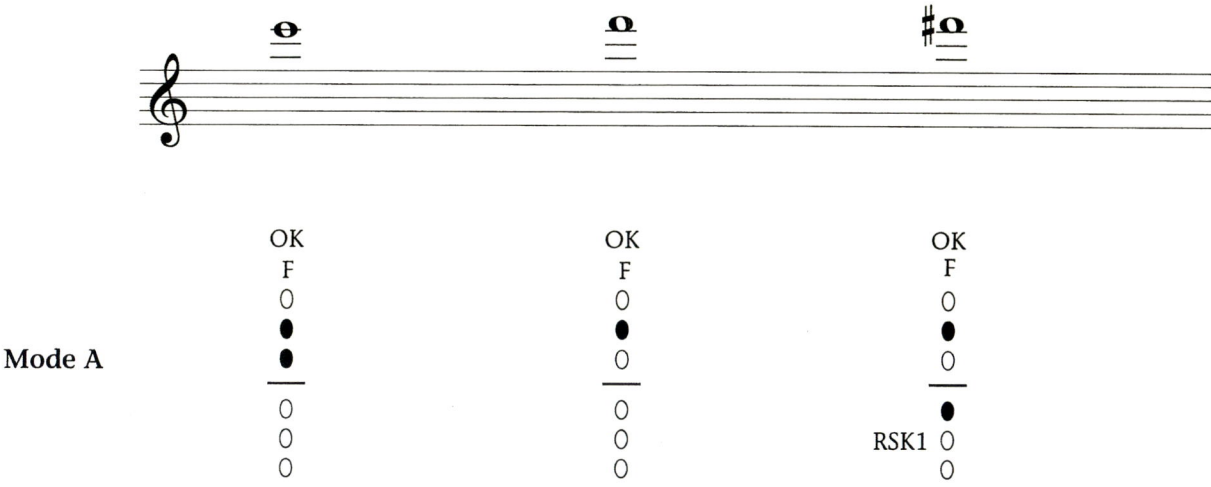

Mode A

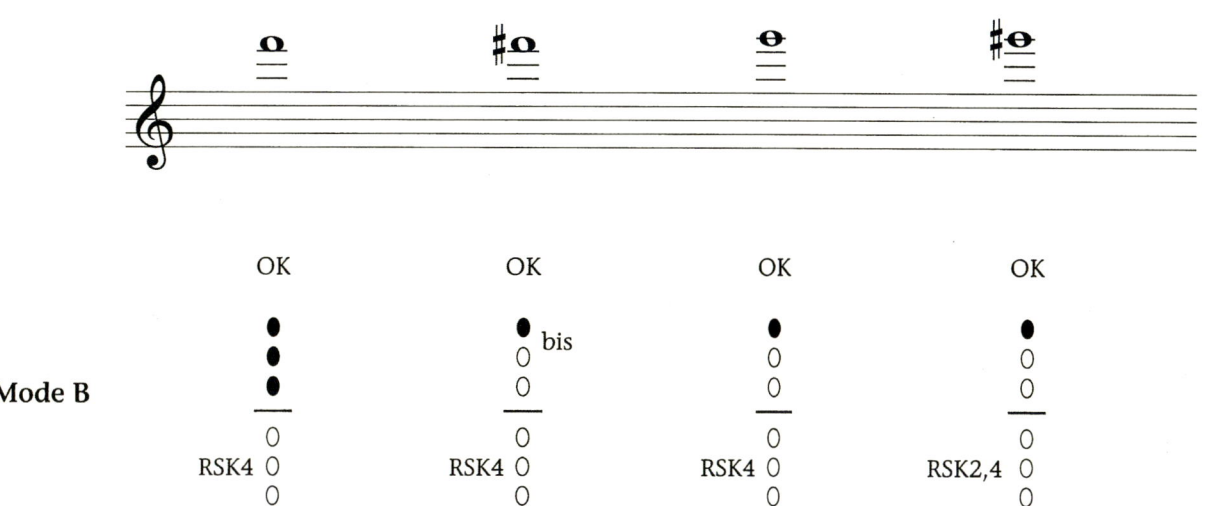

Mode B

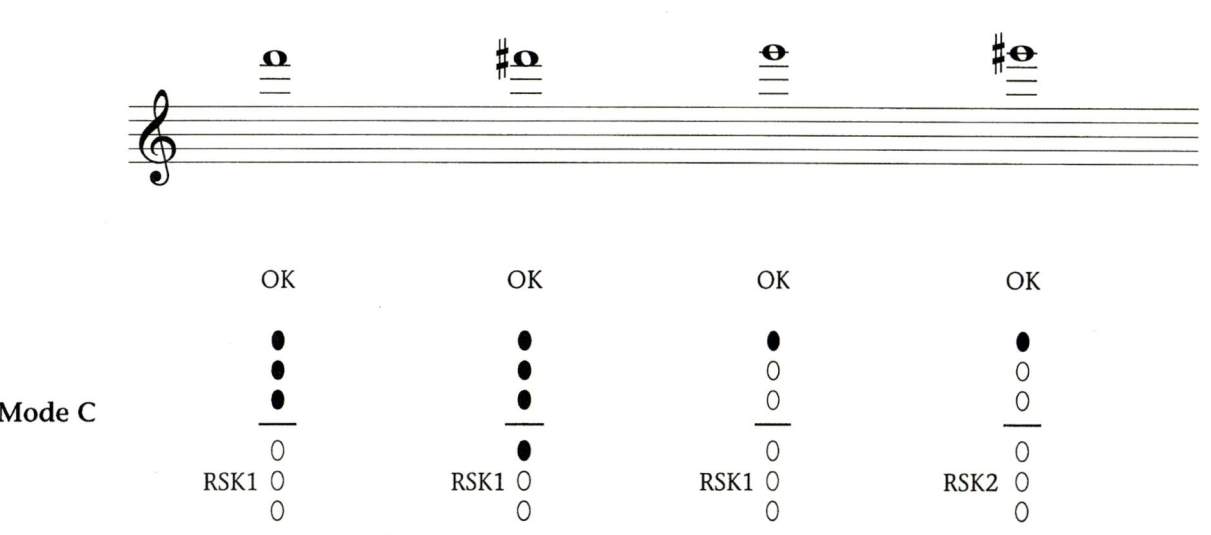

Mode C

Bridging the Registers

The following examples for soprano, alto, and tenor are useful in bridging the normal high register to the above-normal range. Use fingerings from Mode A for all examples.

Soprano, Alto, and Tenor:

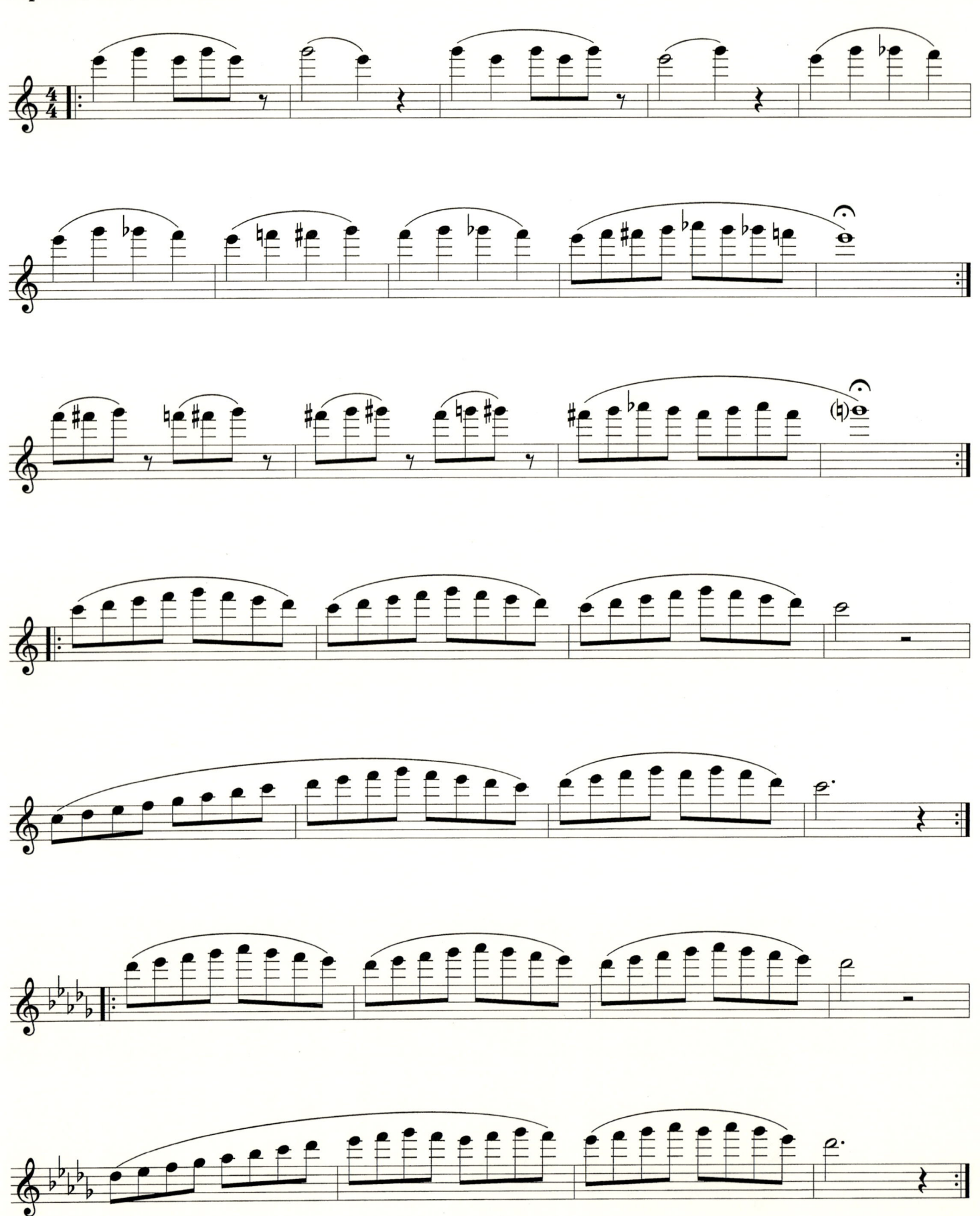

Soprano, Alto, and Tenor:

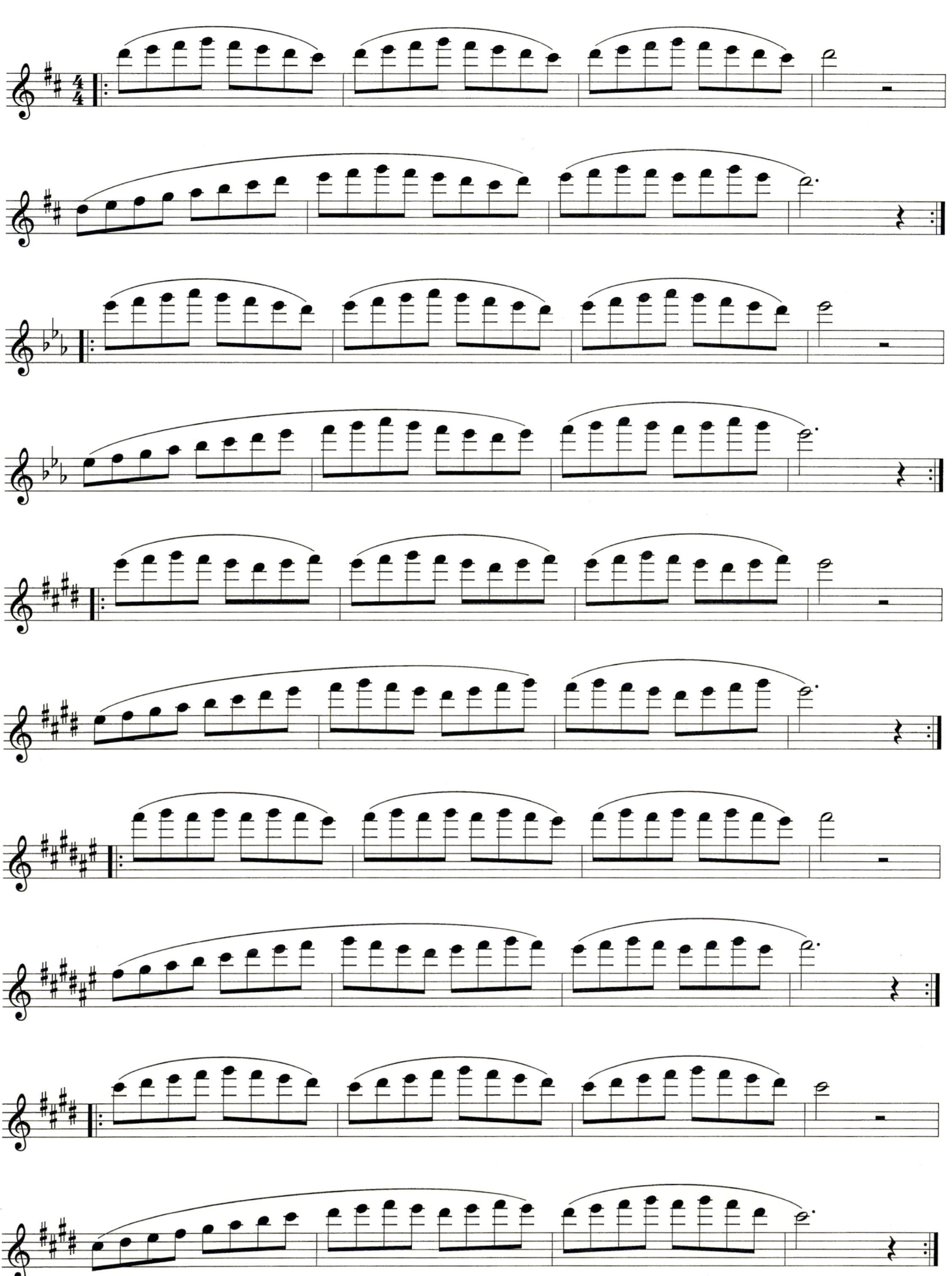

Soprano, Alto, and Tenor:

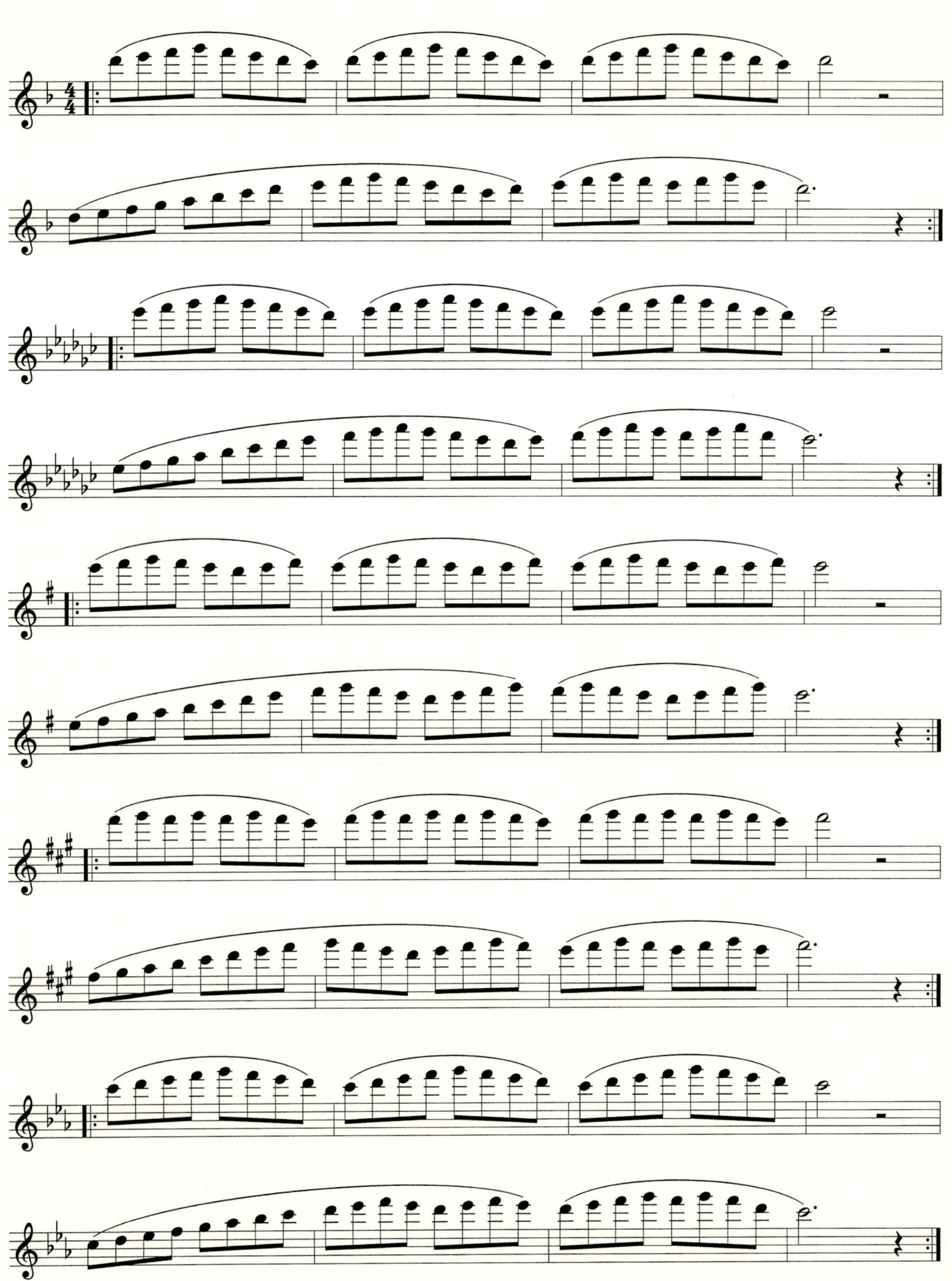

Soprano, Alto, and Tenor:

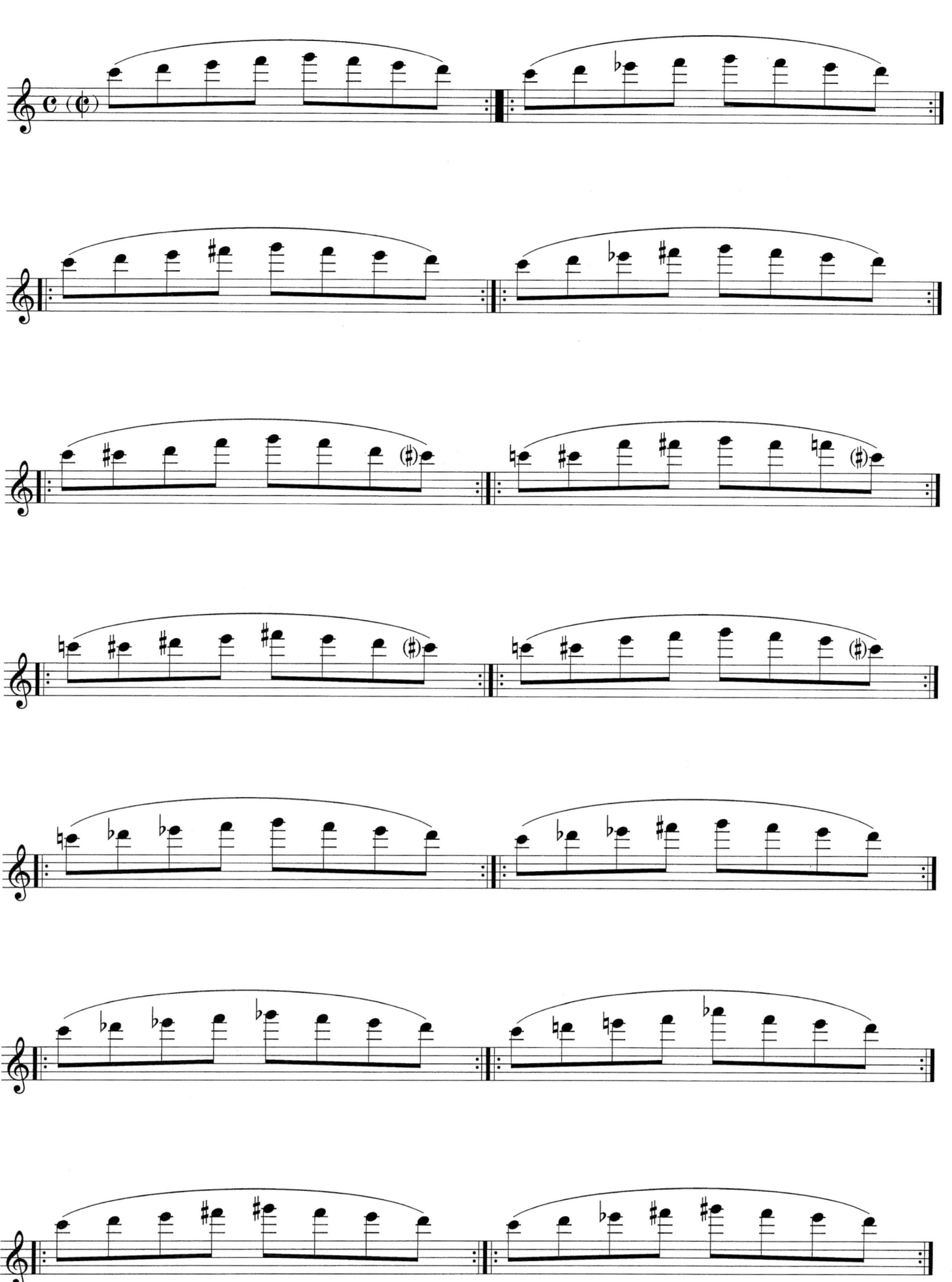

Soprano, Alto, and Tenor:

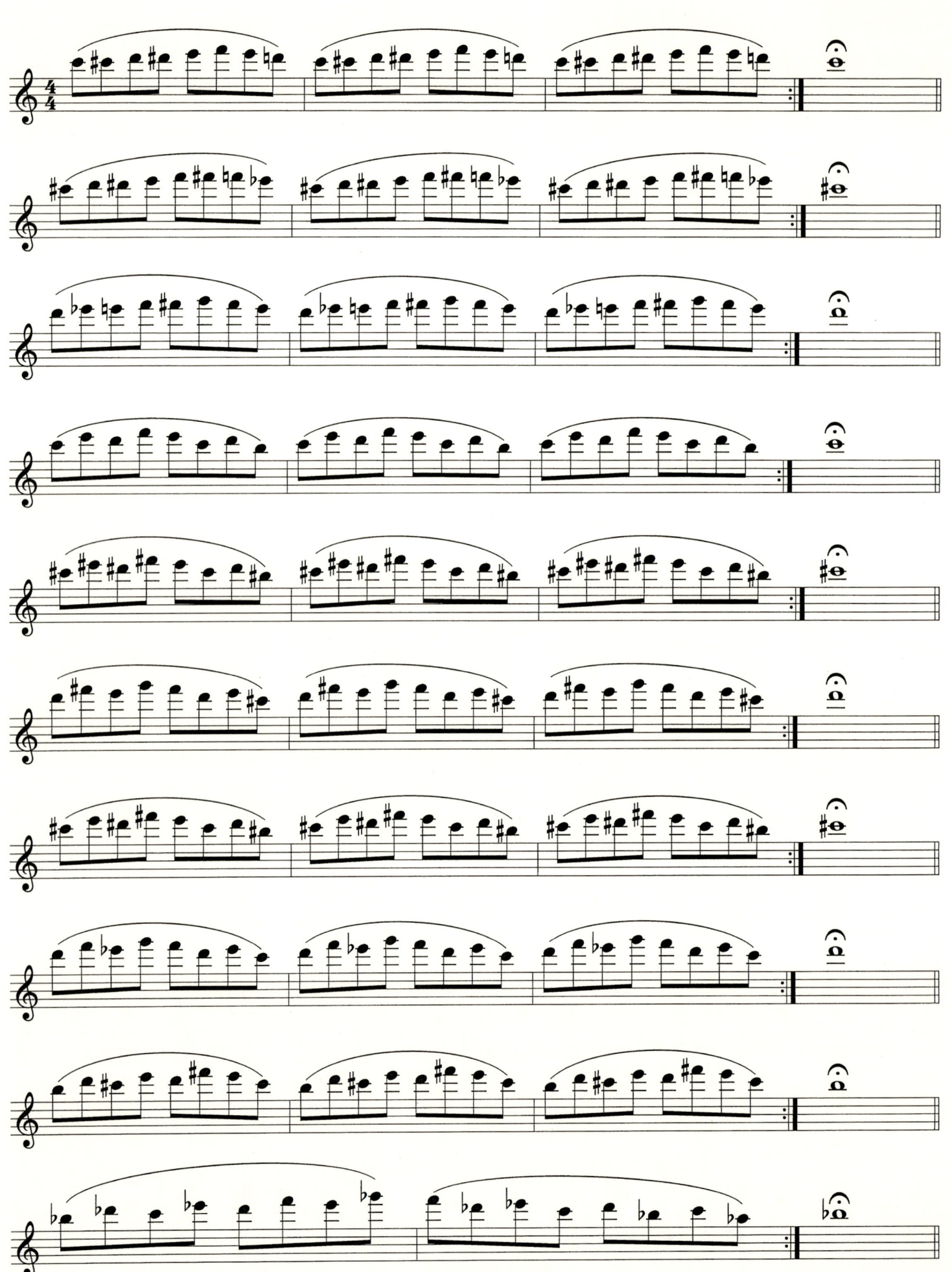

Combining Modes for Practical Solutions

Below are examples for alto saxophone where two or more modes can be combined to obtain the optimal result. In examples where the bracket ([ ) is used allow the left index finger to open key F (front F Key), while keeping it in the normal position for B. This affords a smooth transition among modes.

Examples for Alto:

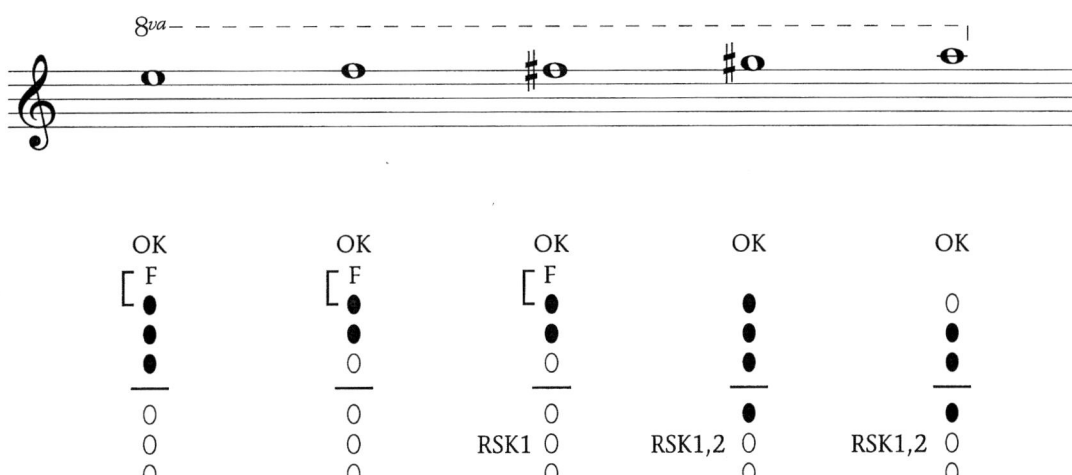

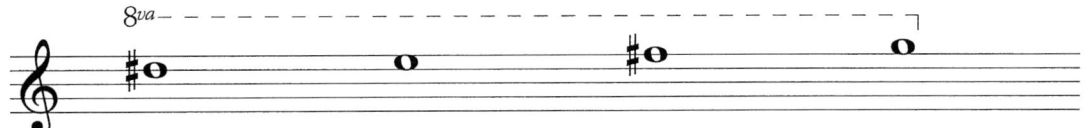

or

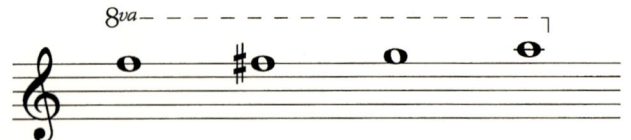
or

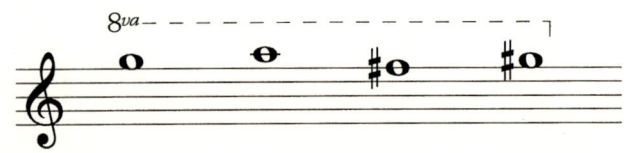
or

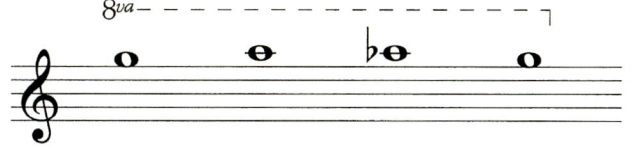
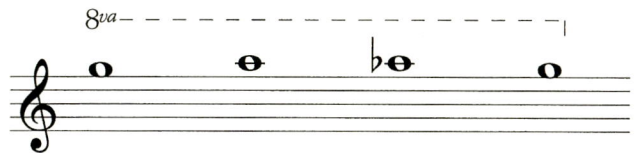

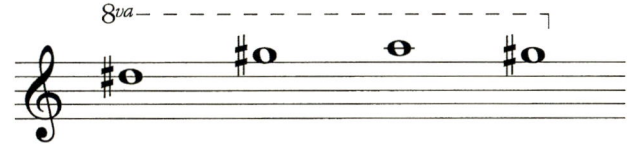
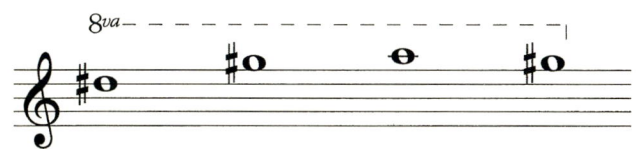

Beyond the Sixths

After gaining a familiarity with overblowing a sixth higher, the procedure may be expanded to include a fourth higher yielding the following:

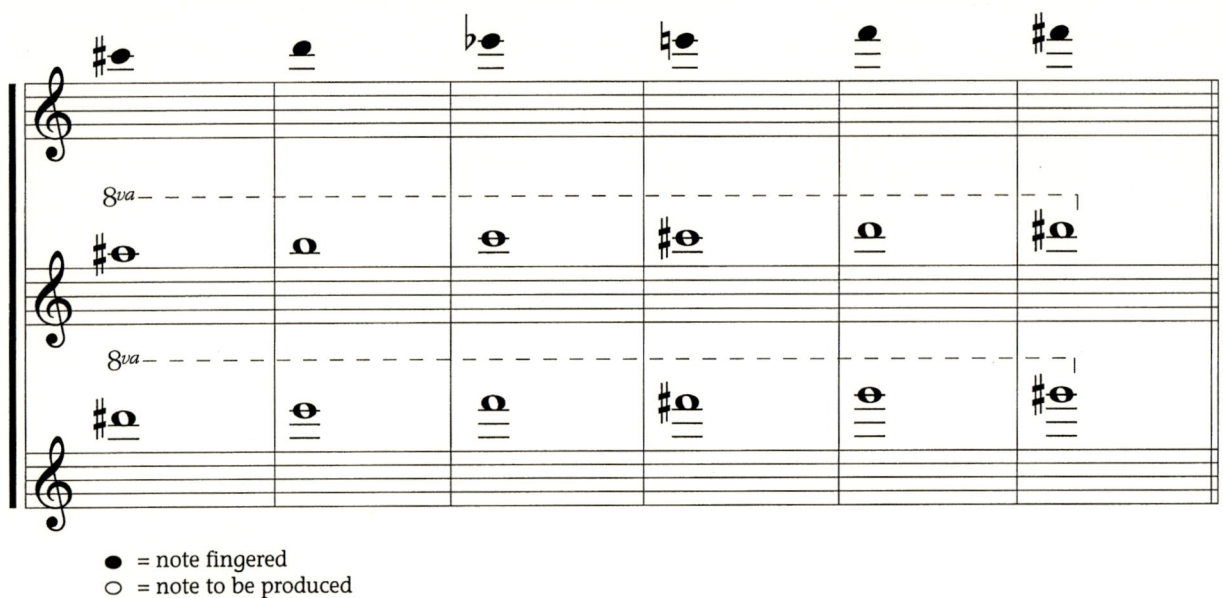

● = note fingered
○ = note to be produced

For Baritone the pattern becomes:

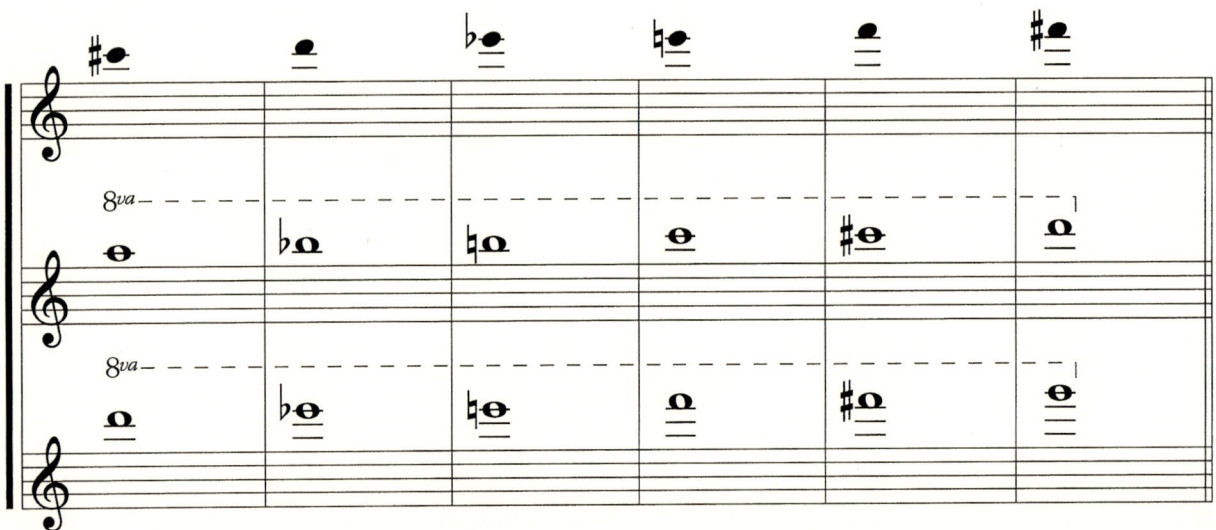

For tones above and including [notation] it is necessary for most players to make a significant embouchure change. The amount of lip over the lower teeth is greatly decreased—the exact amount to be determined by each performer through daily practice. The reason for such a small amount of lip cushion in the extreme high tones is due to the tremendously high frequencies and the corresponding need for increasingly faster vibrations of the reed itself.

Soprano, Alto, and Tenor:

Baritone:

36

FINGERING CHART FOR THE HIGH TONES
For Soprano, Alto, Tenor, and Baritone Saxophones

There is no "complete" fingering chart for any instrument, and that is especially true for the above-normal range of the saxophone. When using the fingerings below, it is important to keep in mind the different modes, and how fingerings relate to each other: tone, response, intonation, facility. Success in playing the high tones will be achieved more easily when embouchure and use of air are understood. It also helps greatly to practice any fingering combination repeatedly without playing. Abbreviations used are explained on page vi.

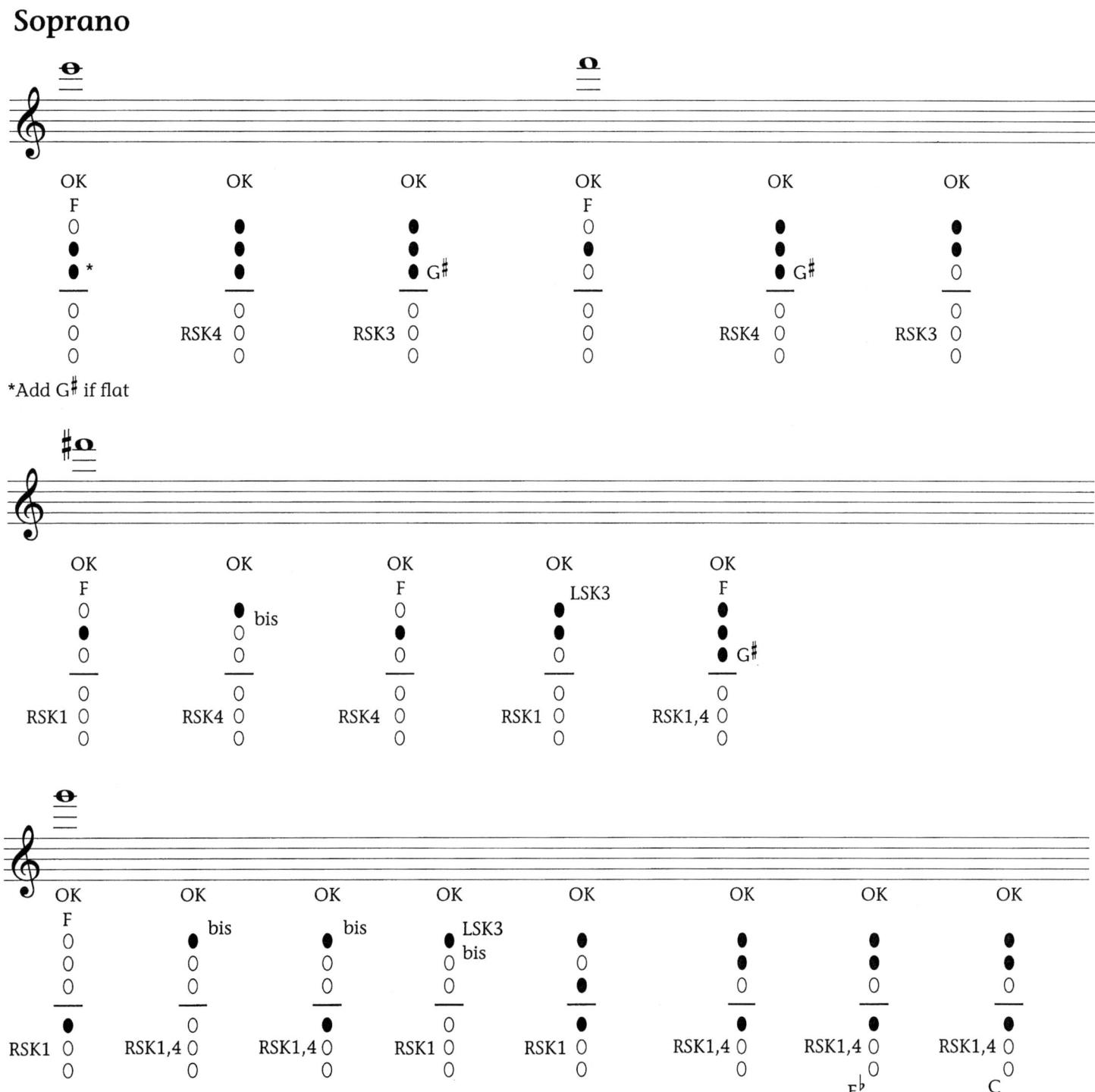

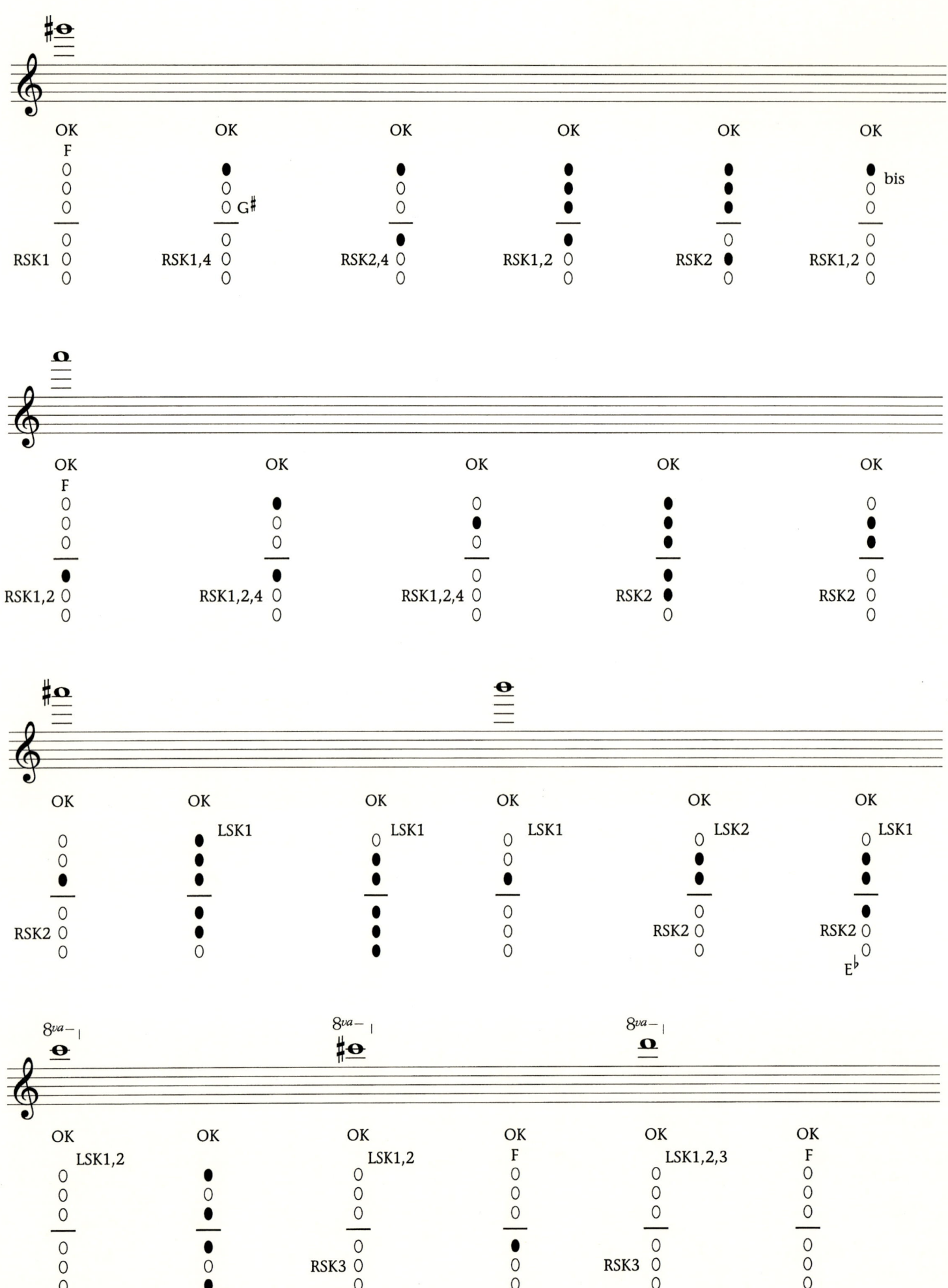

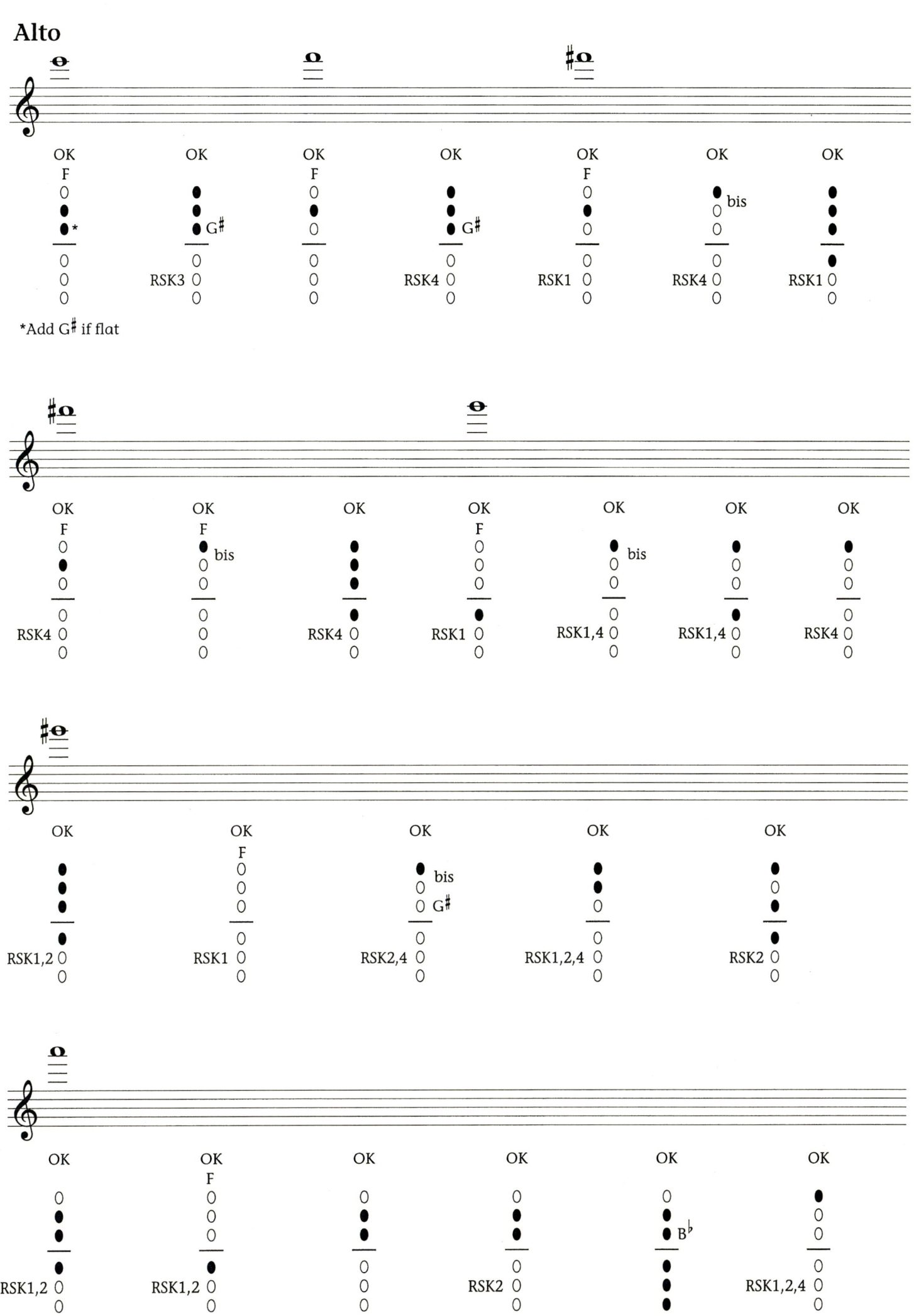

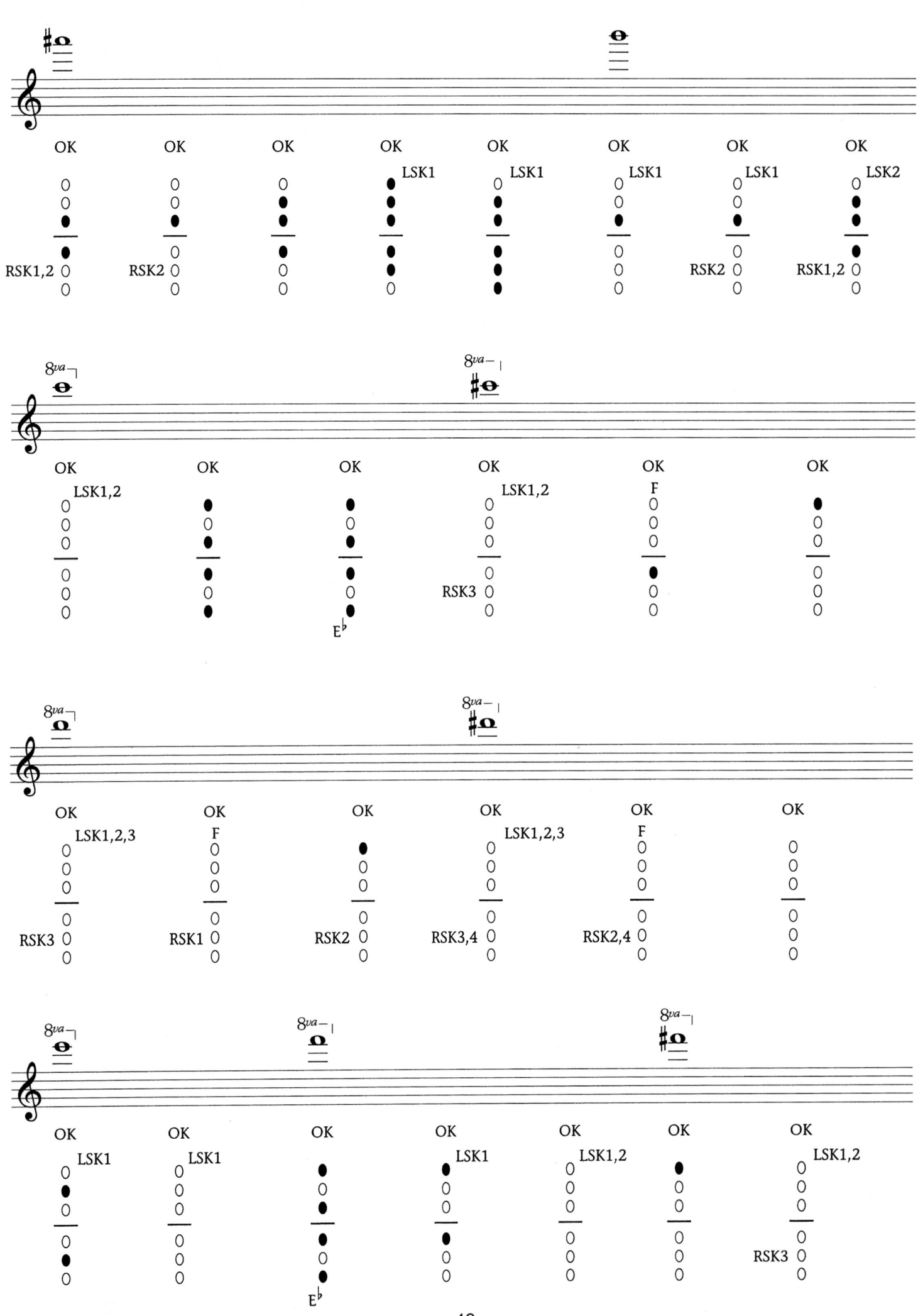

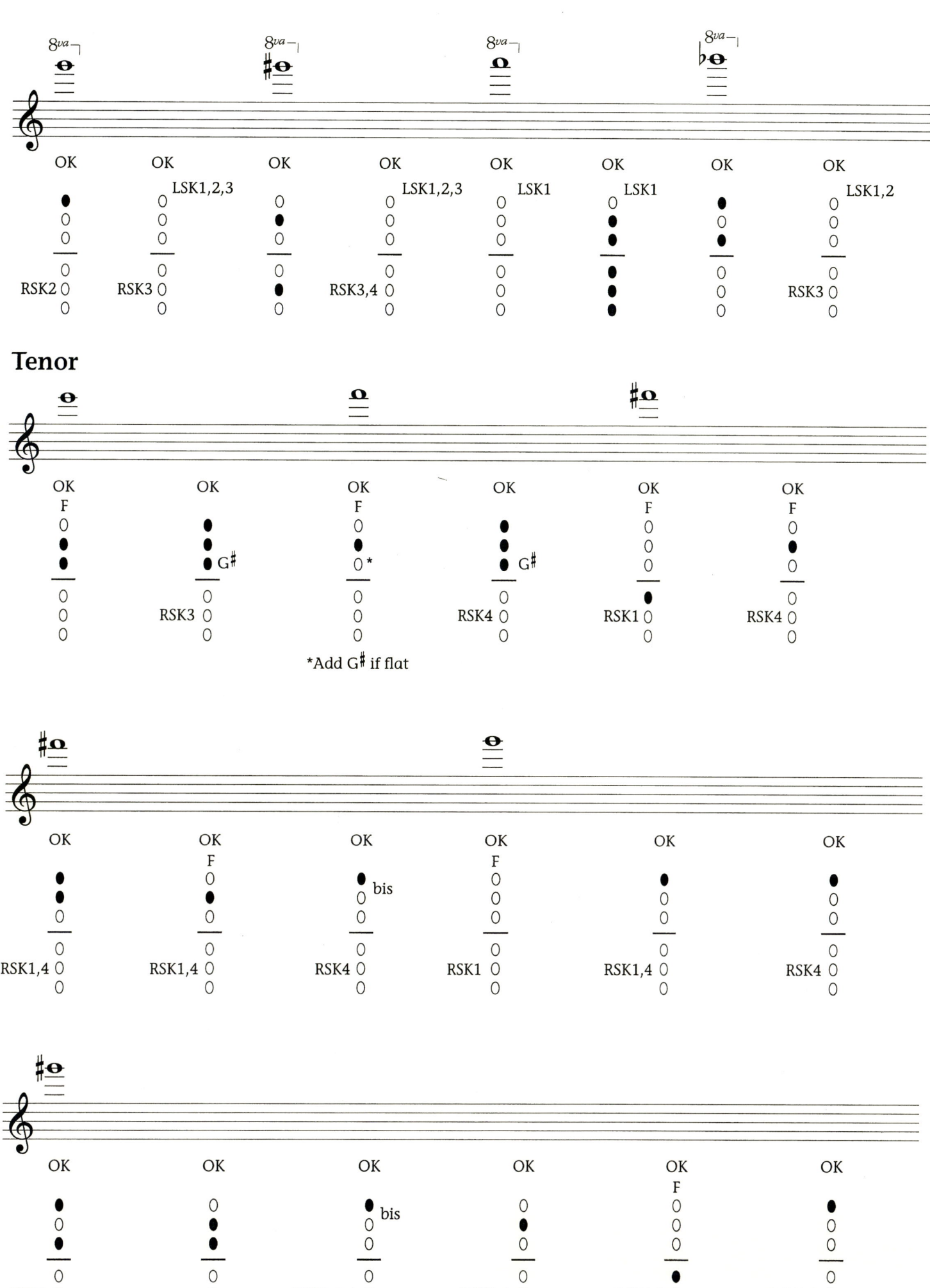

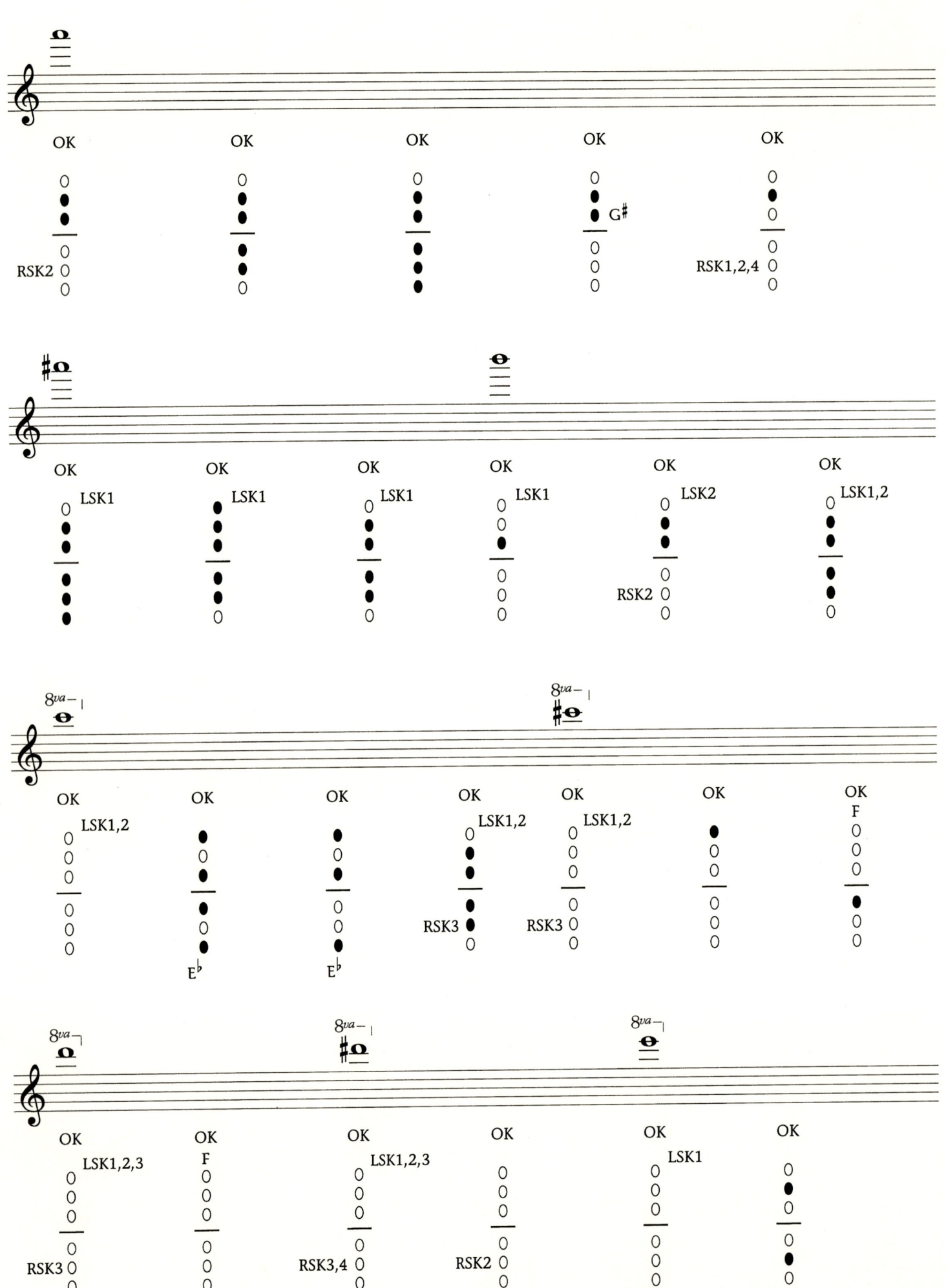

42

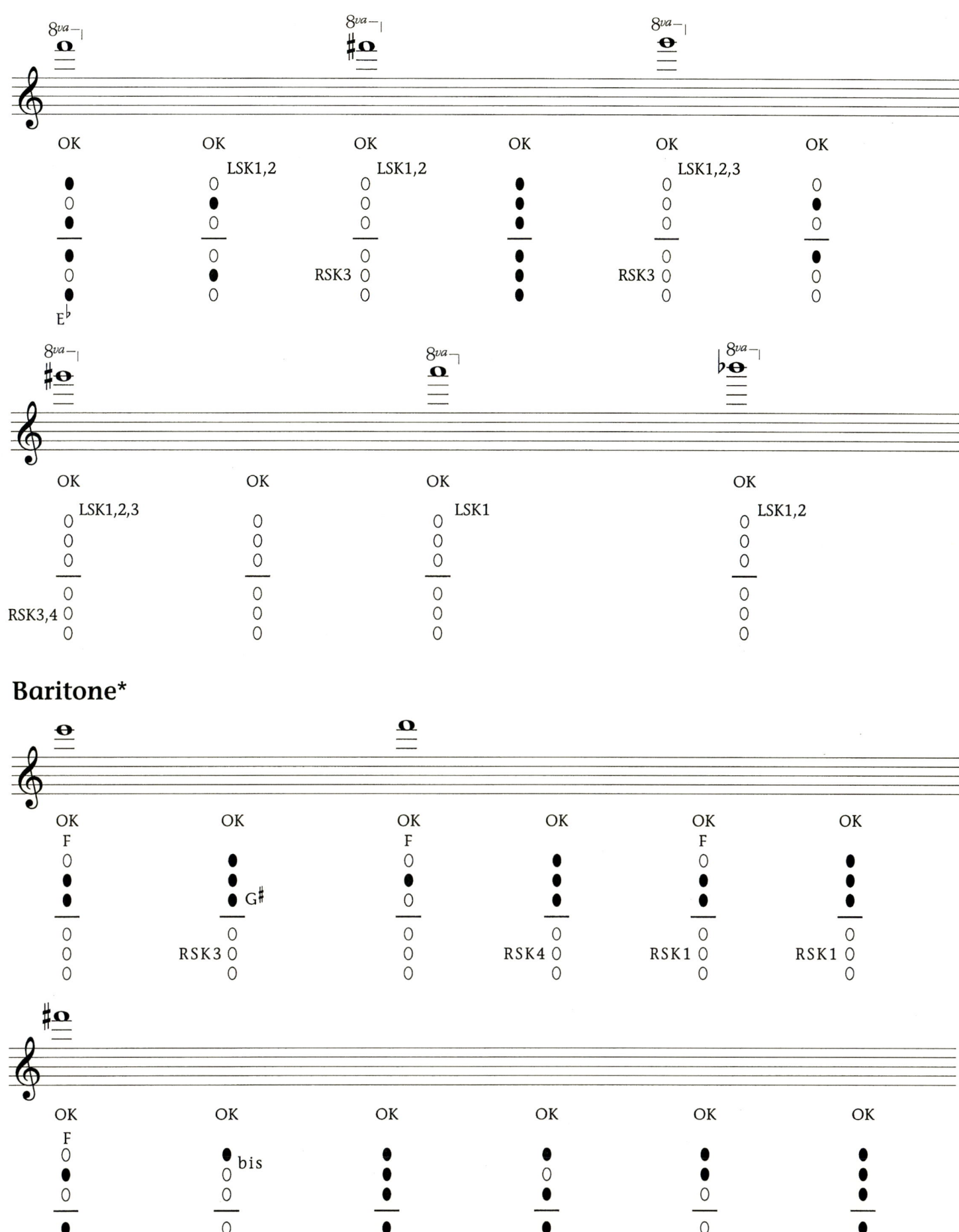

*The author is indebted to Karl Hartman for his verification of the fingerings for baritone saxophone.

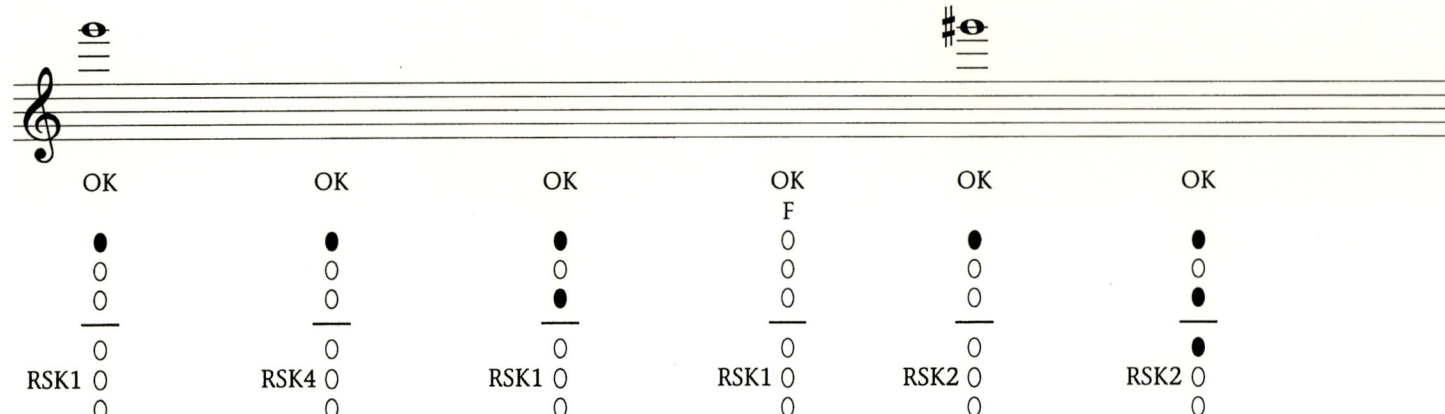
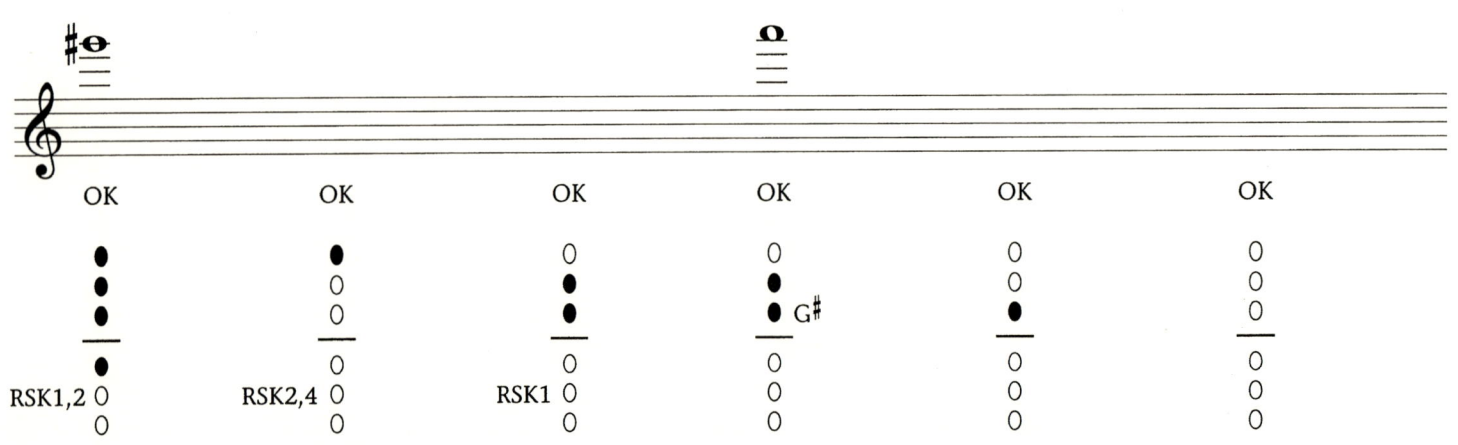
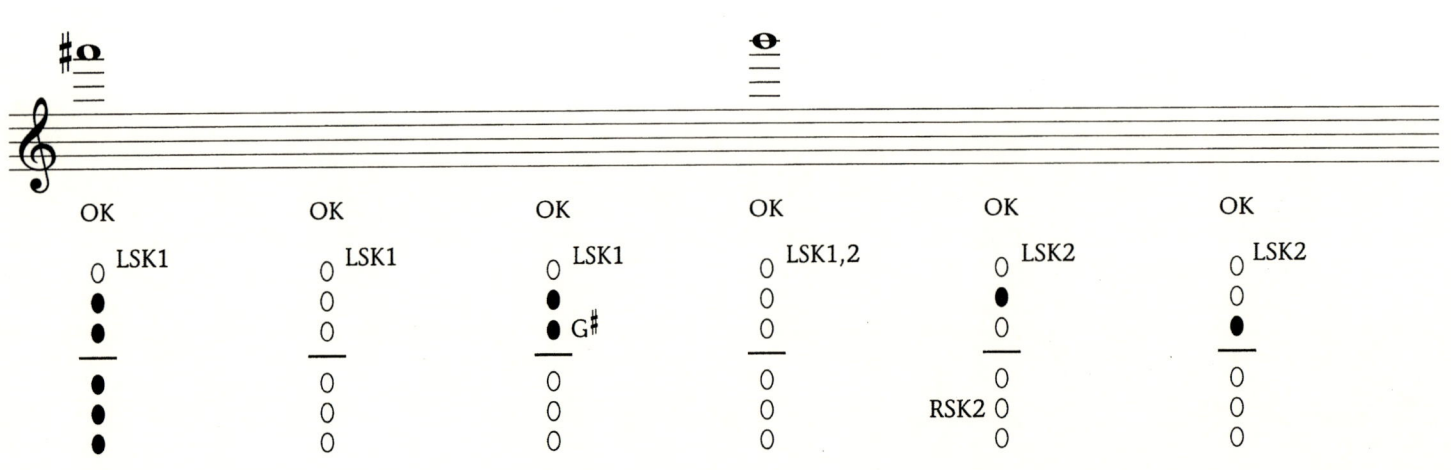

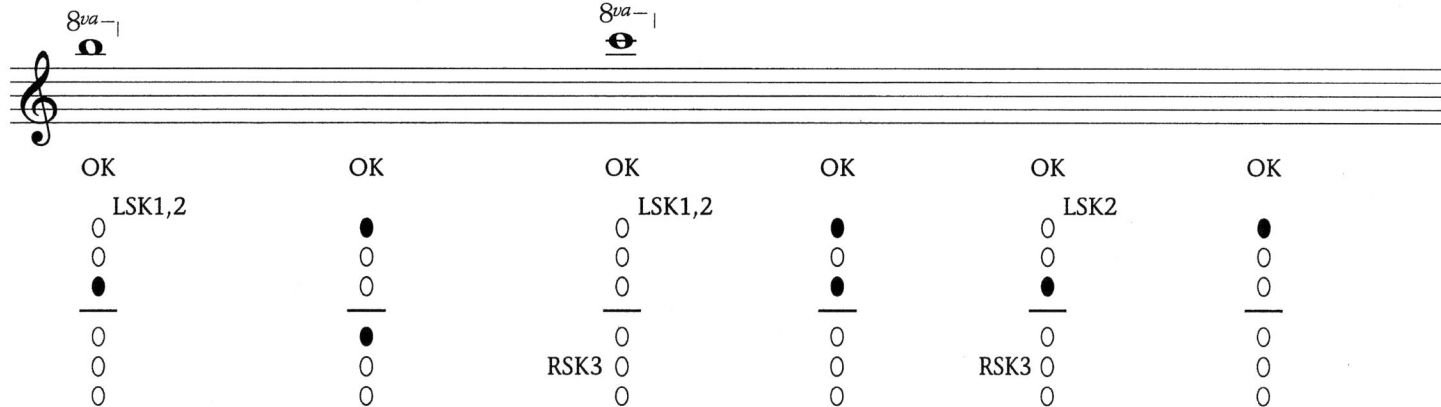
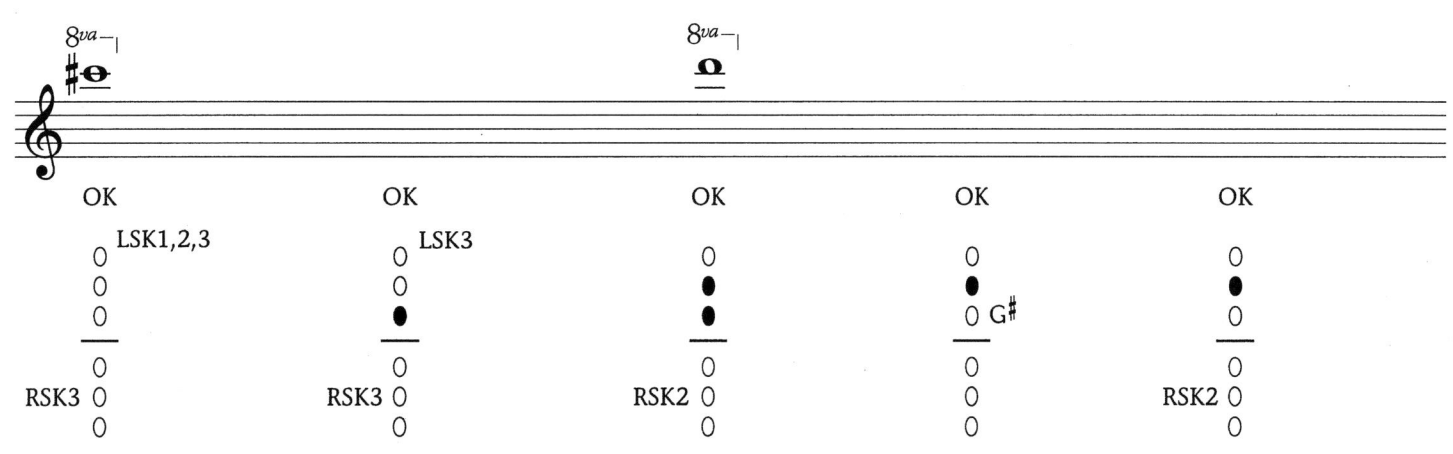
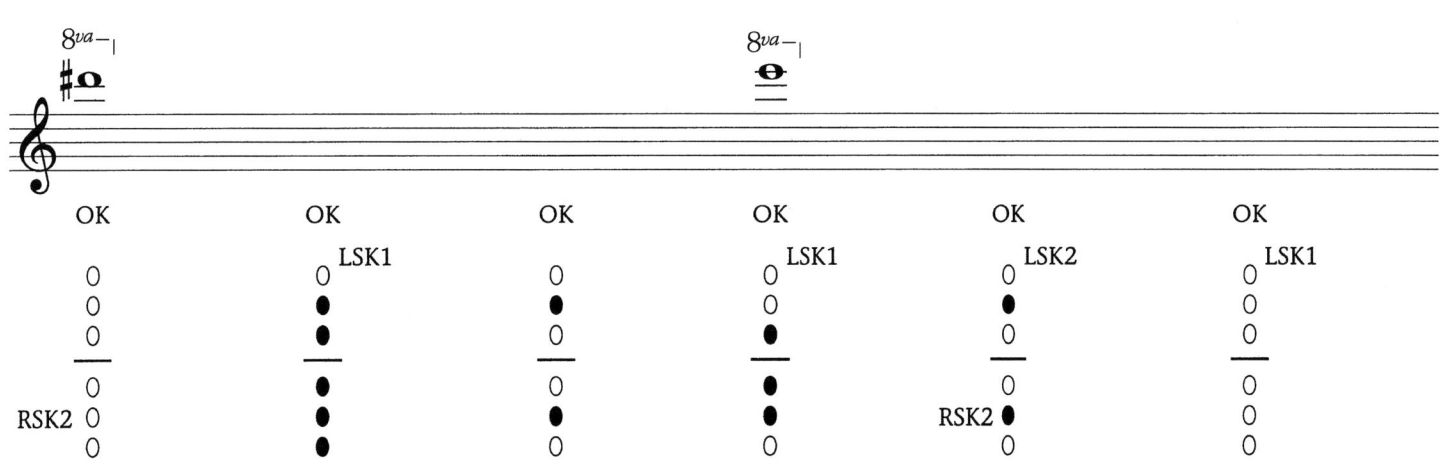

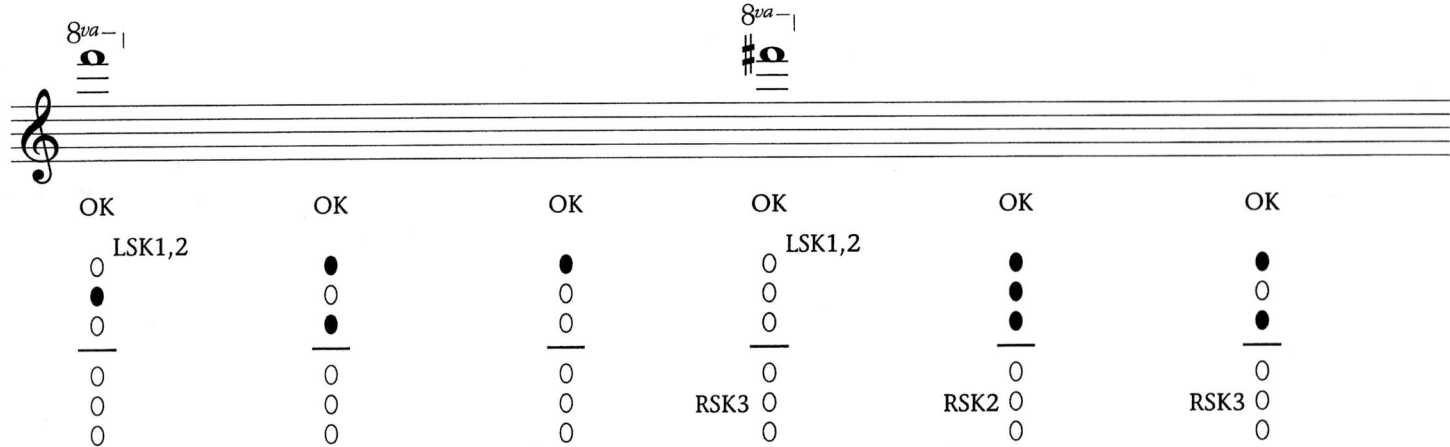
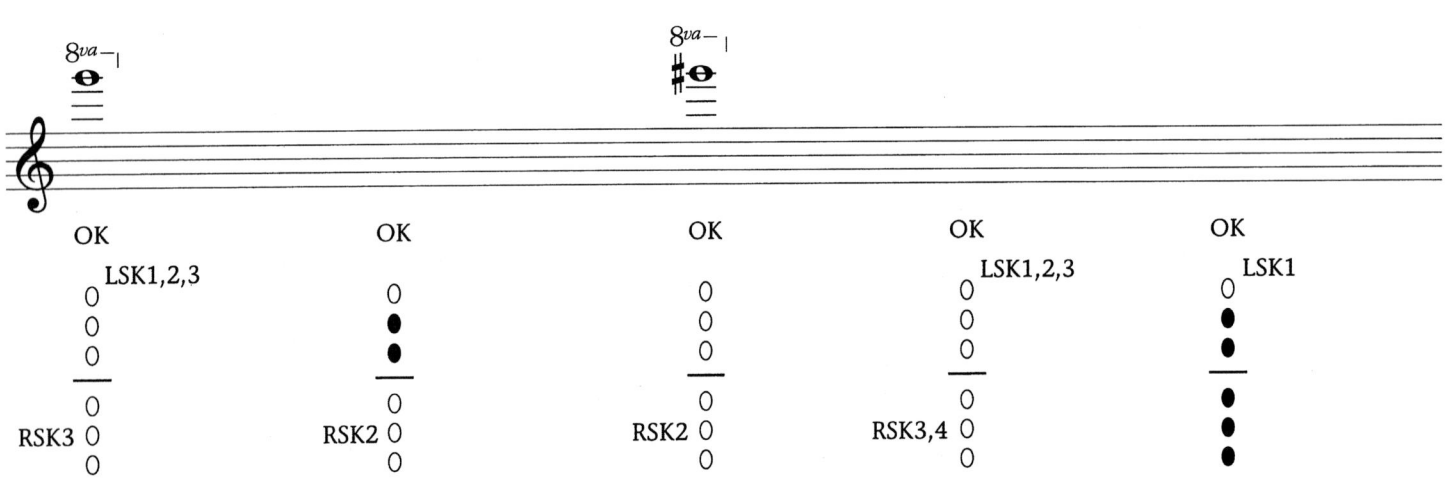
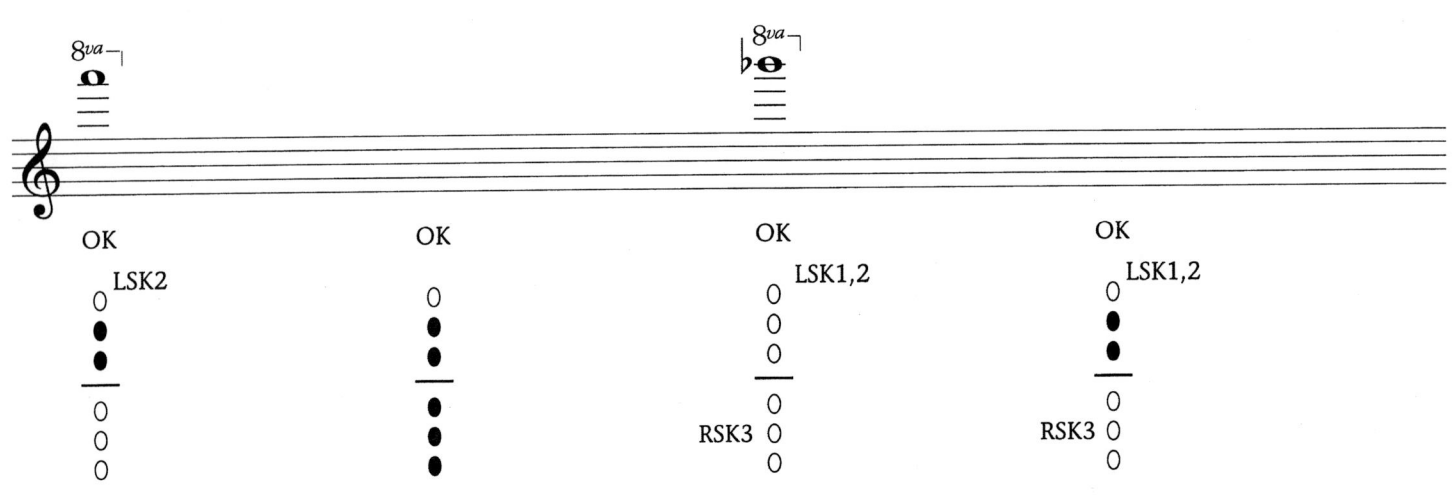

HIGH TONE EXERCISES

Chromatic Patterns: *Use as many combinations of modes as possible.*

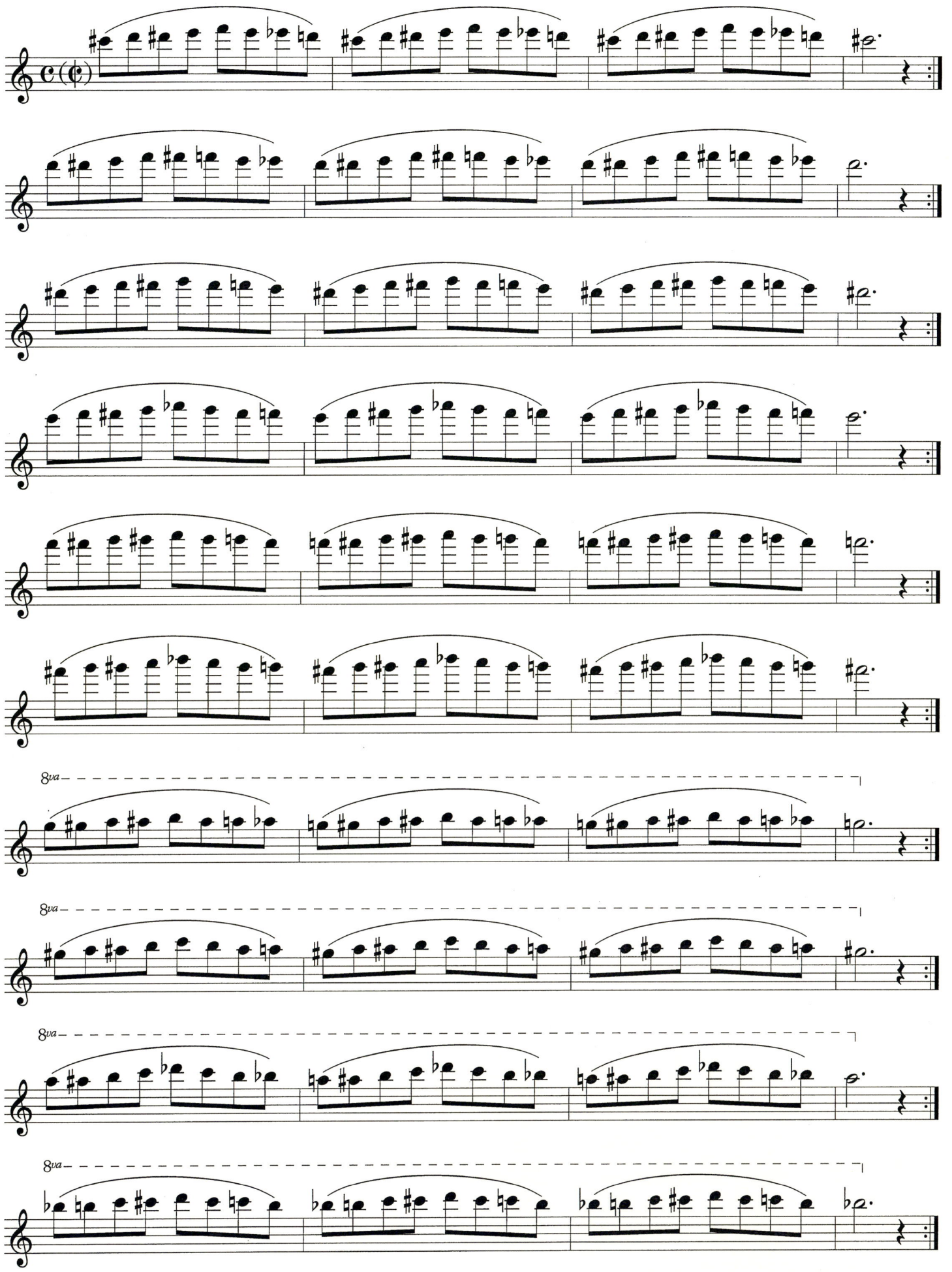

Major Scales: One Octave
Use as many combinations of modes as possible.

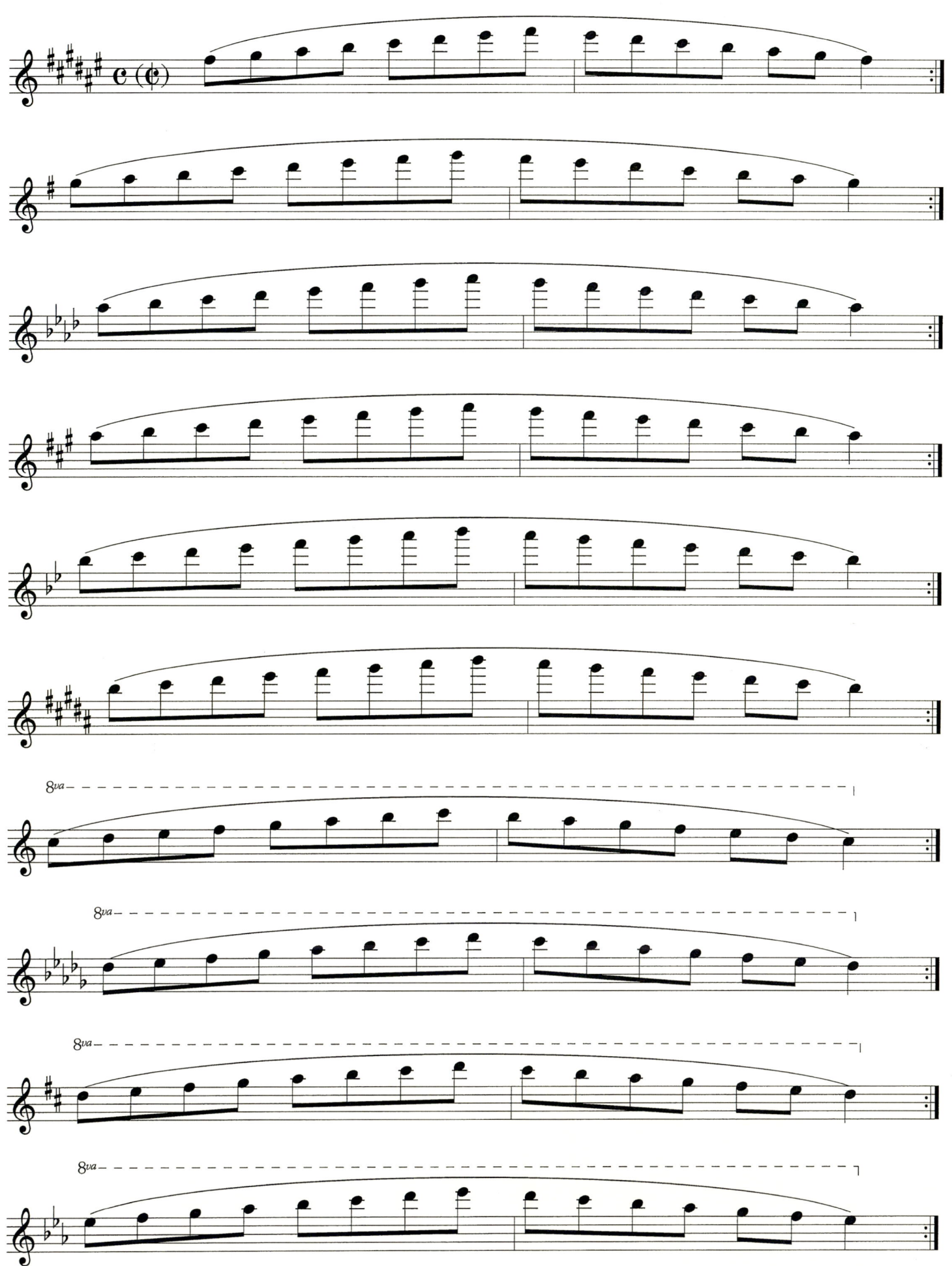

Major Scales: Extended Range *Use as many combinations of modes as possible.*

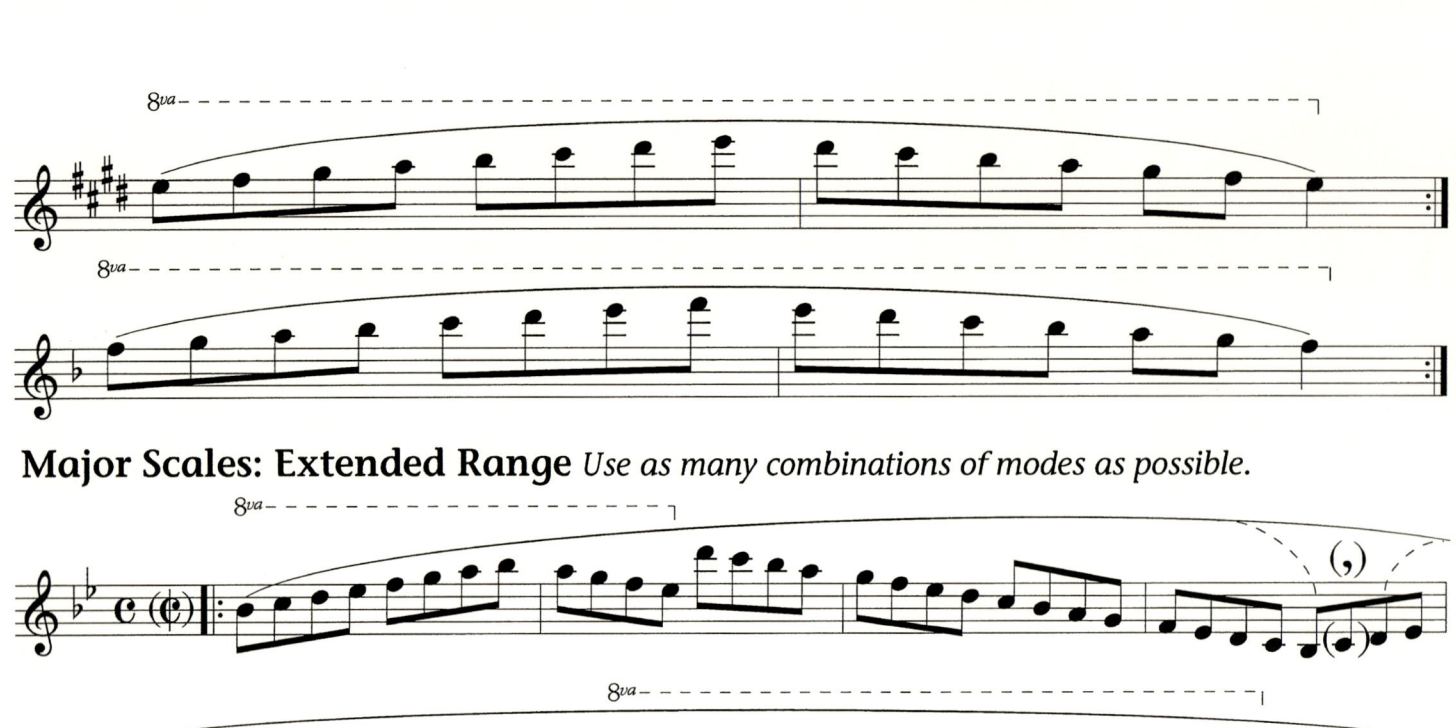

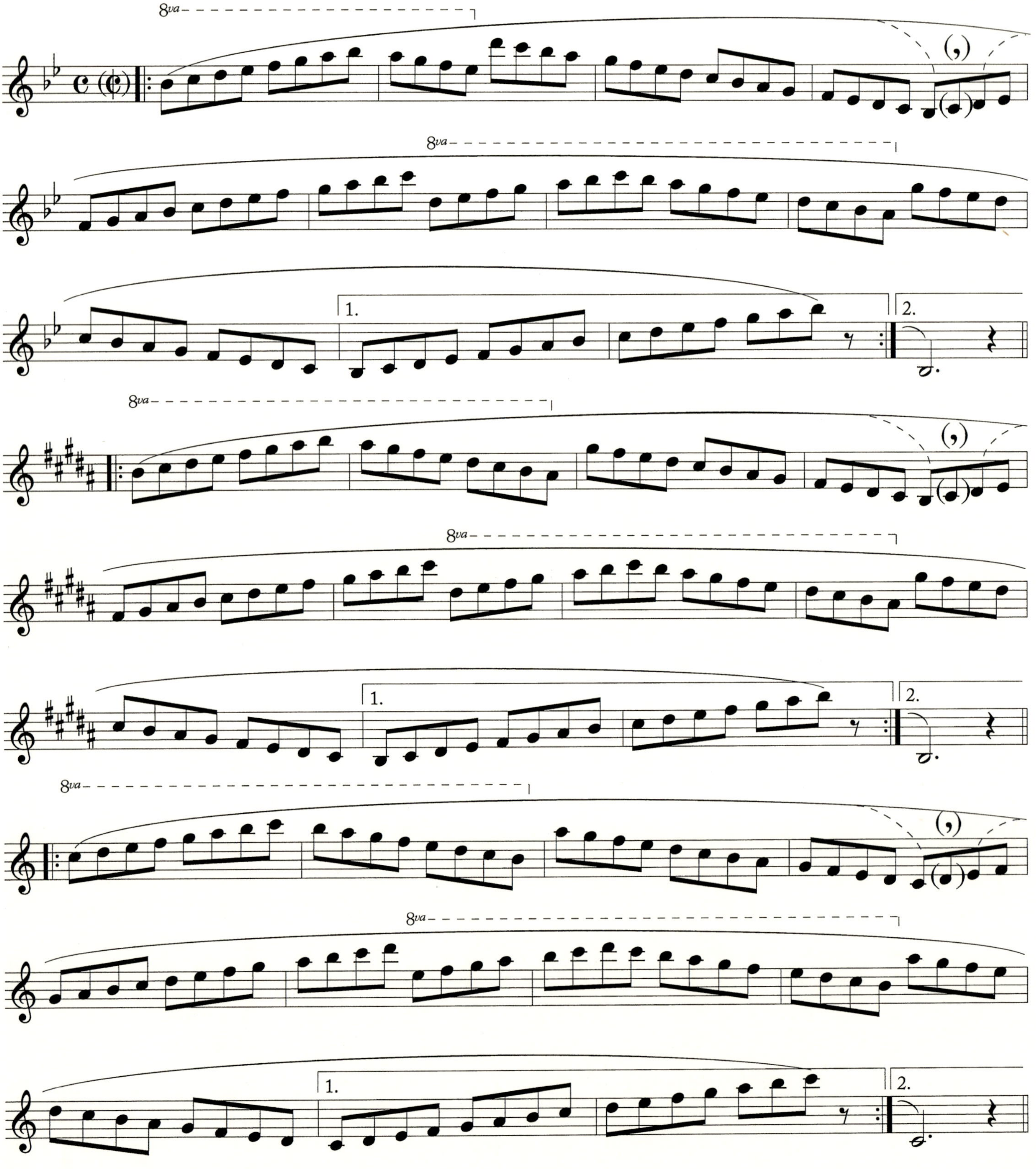

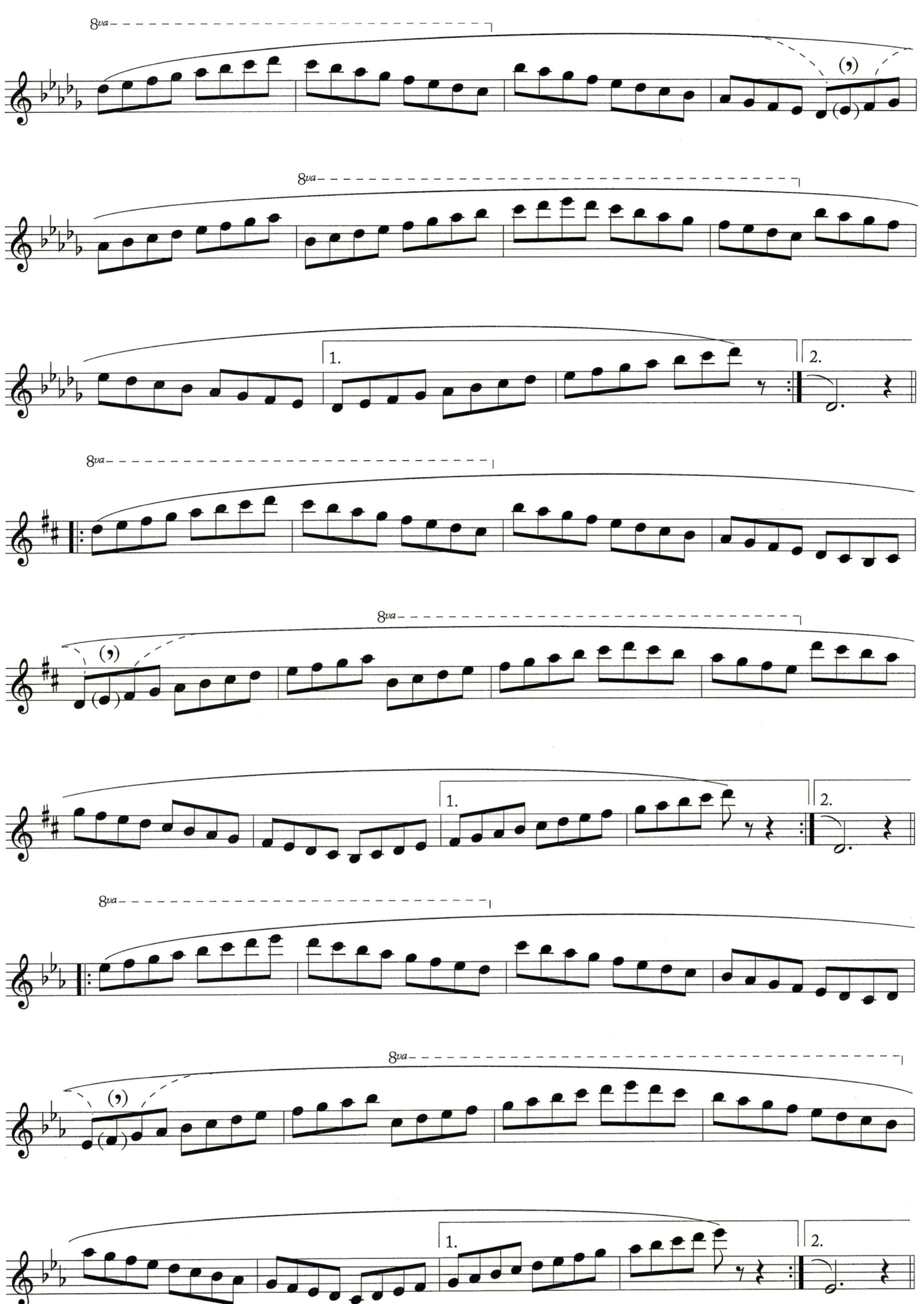

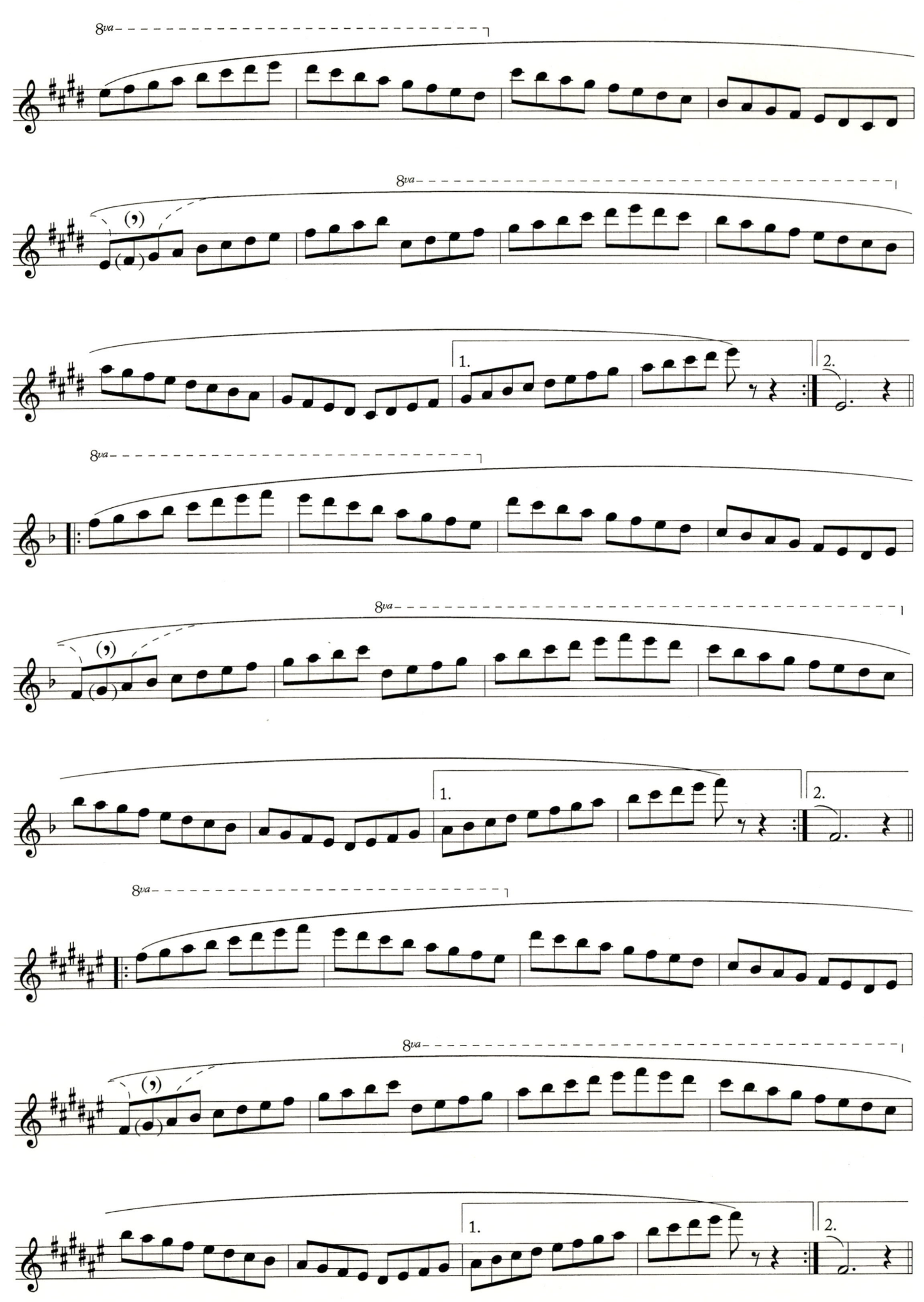

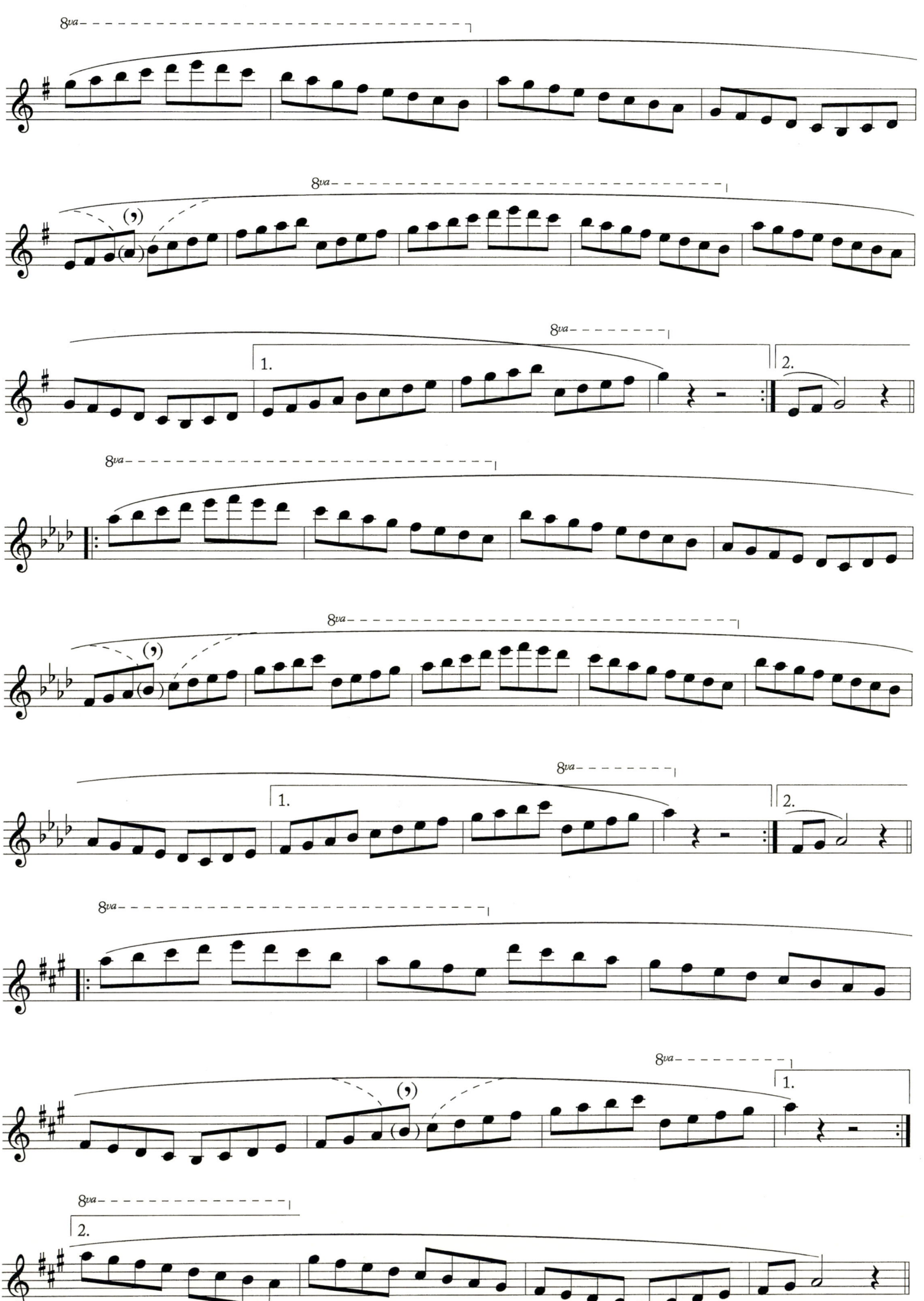

Major Arpeggios

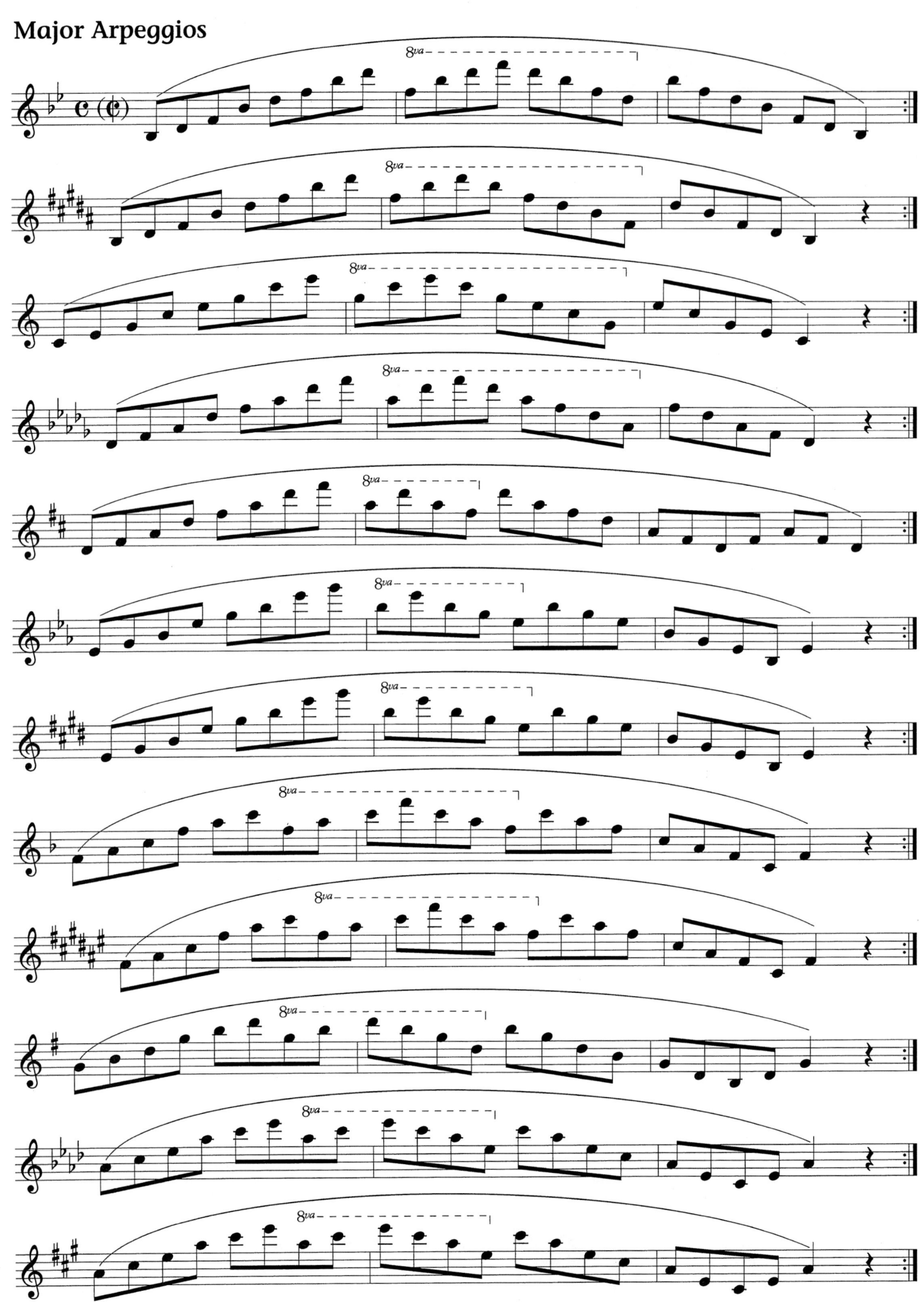

Minor Scales, Harmonic: One Octave
Use as many combinations of modes as possible.

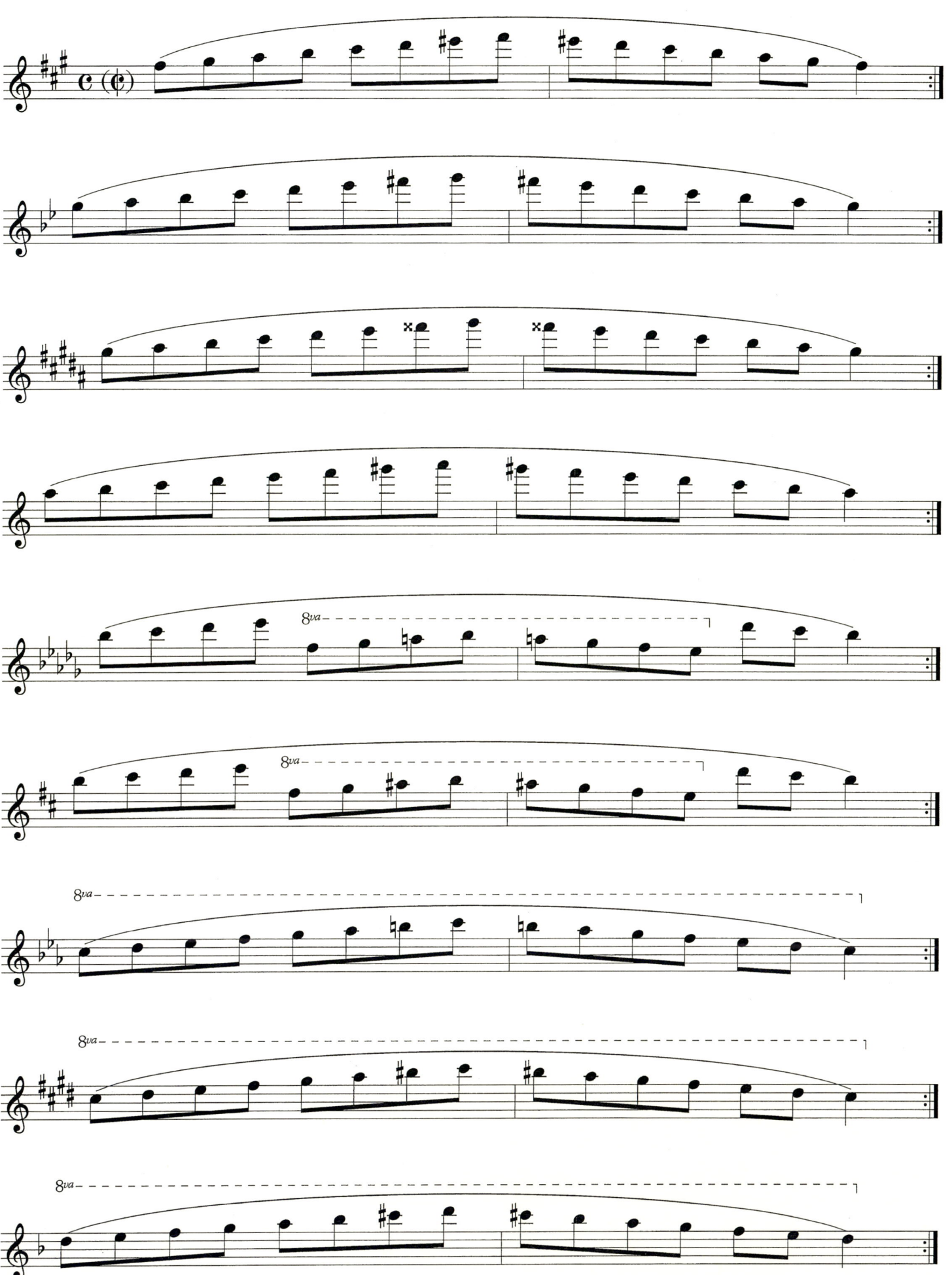

Minor Scales, Harmonic: Extended Range
Use as many combinations of modes as possible.

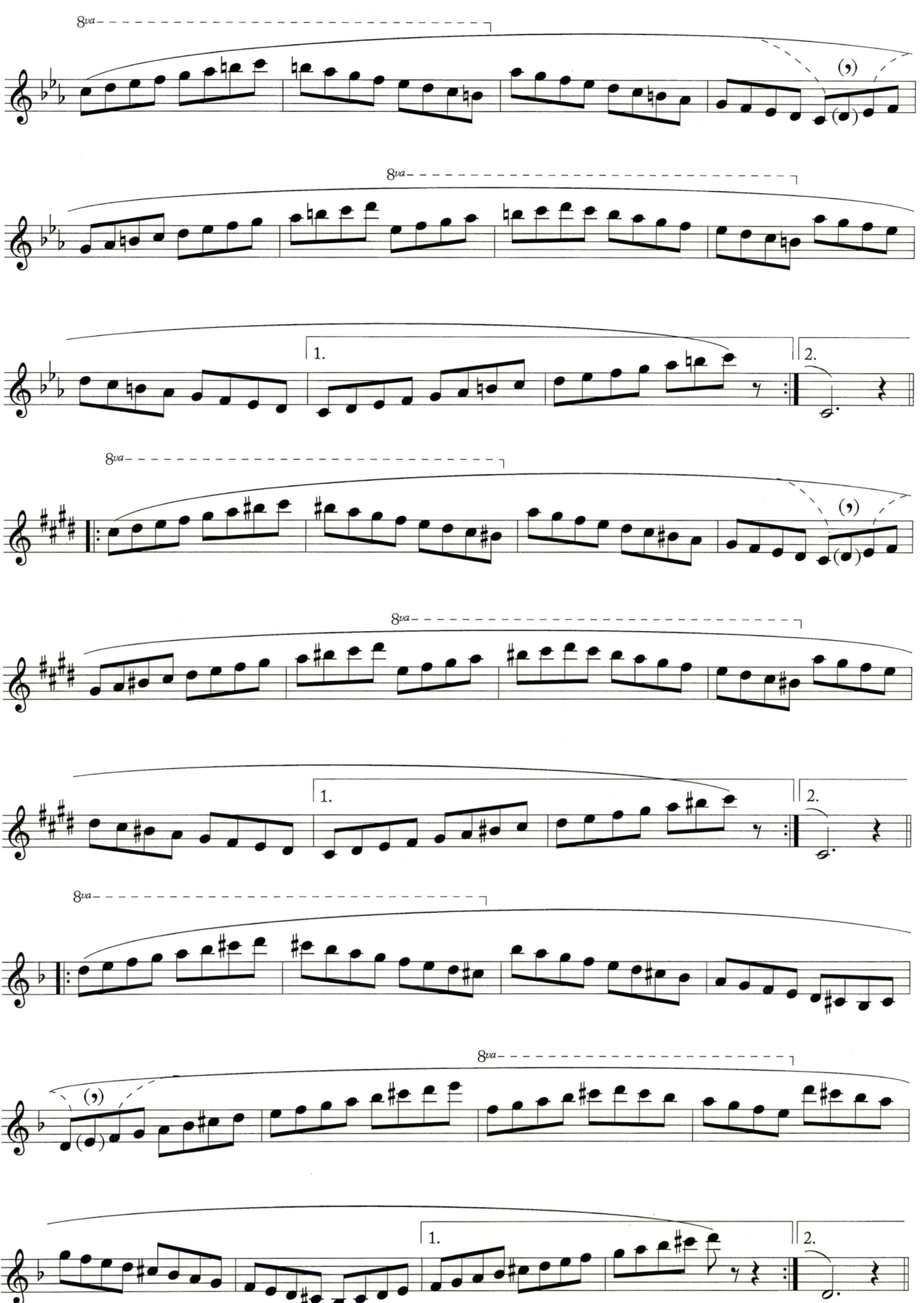

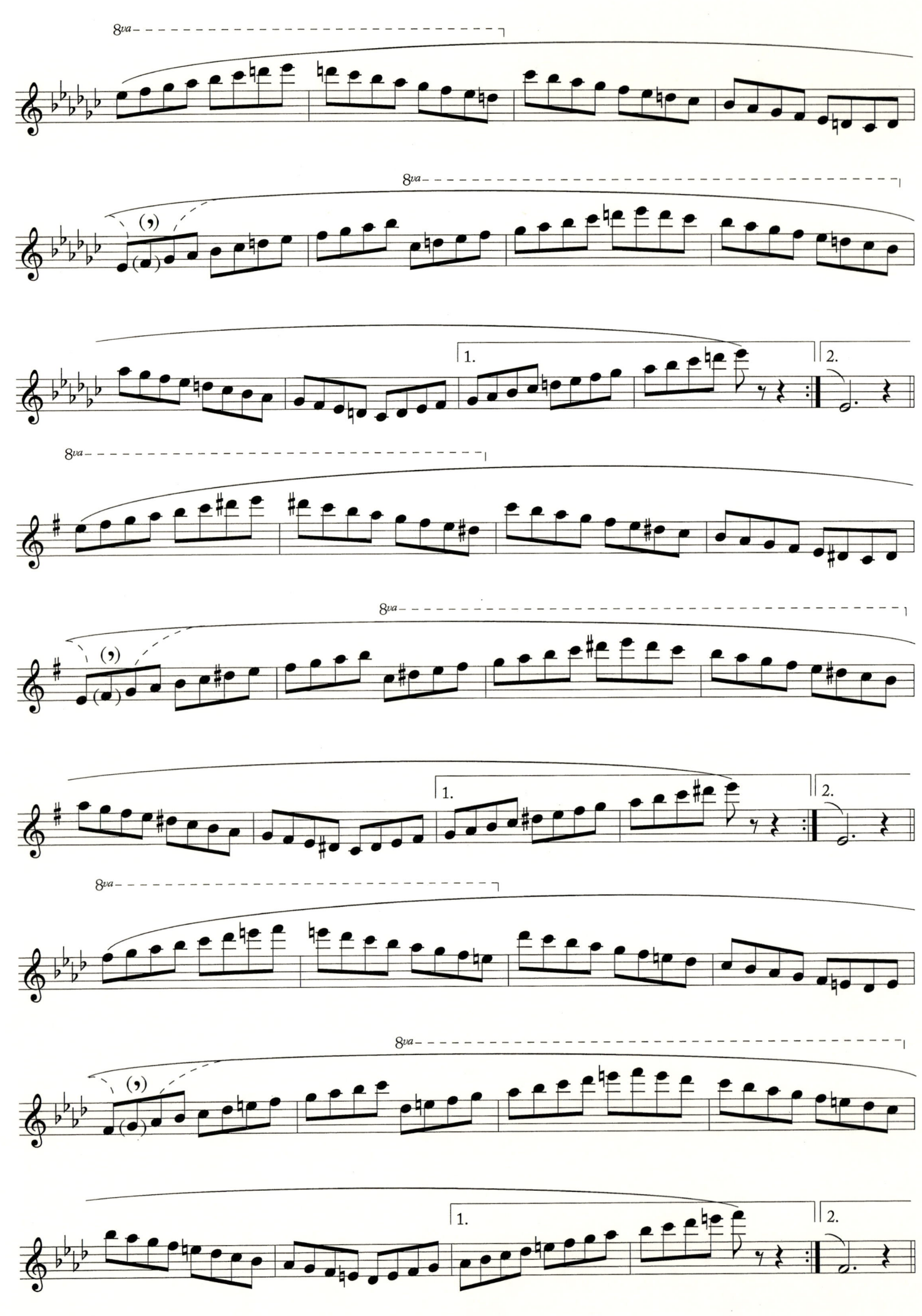

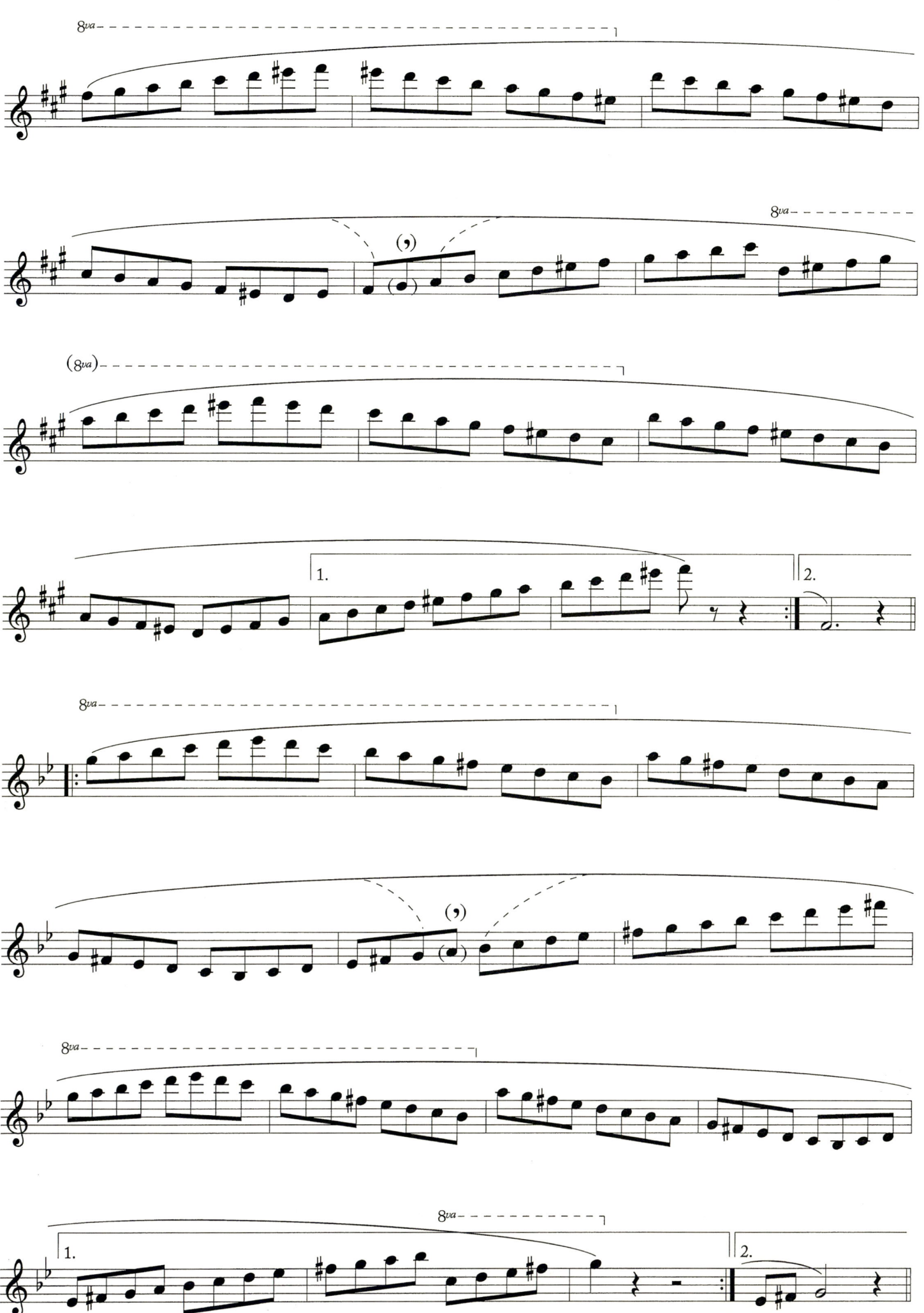

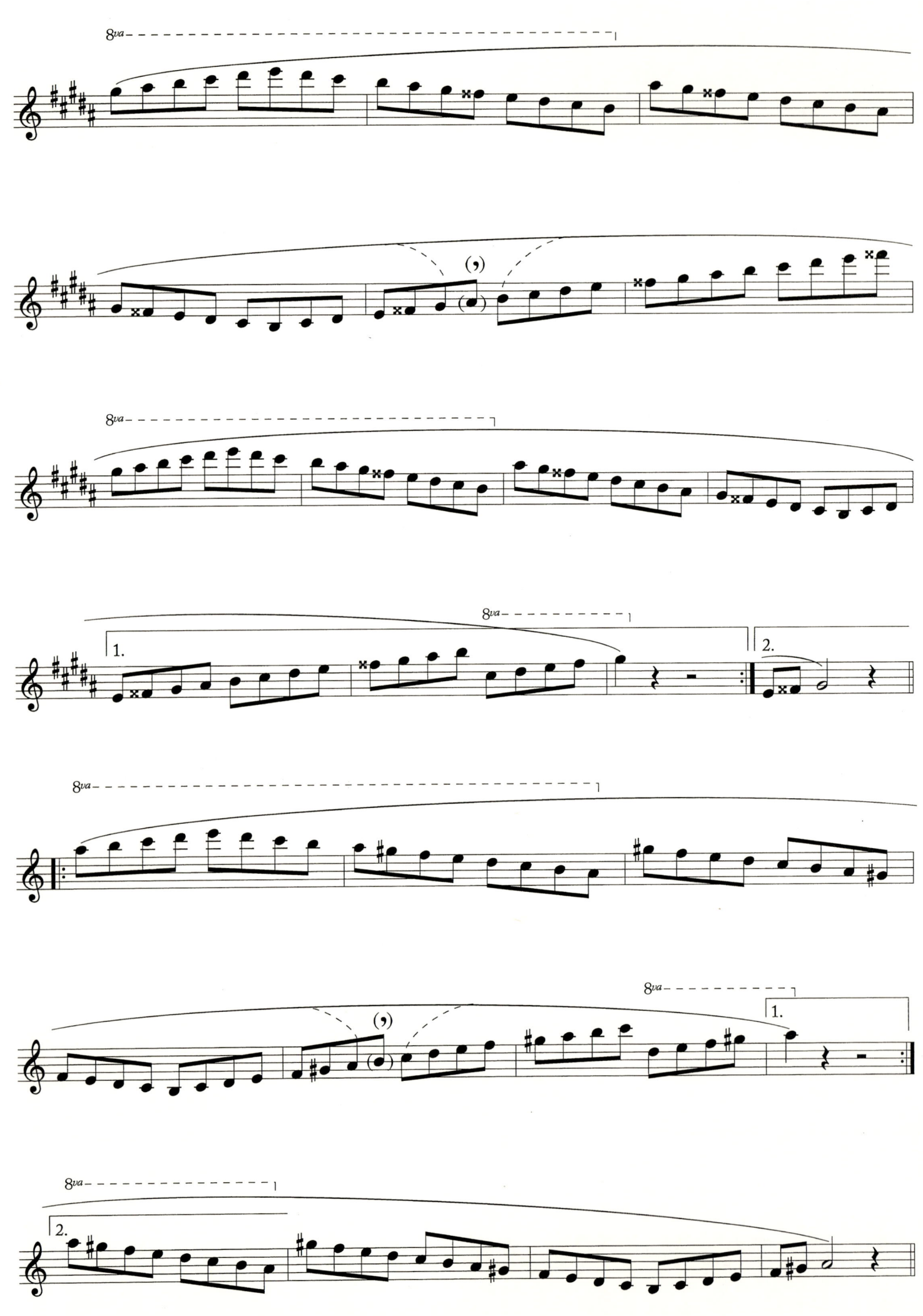

Minor Arpeggios

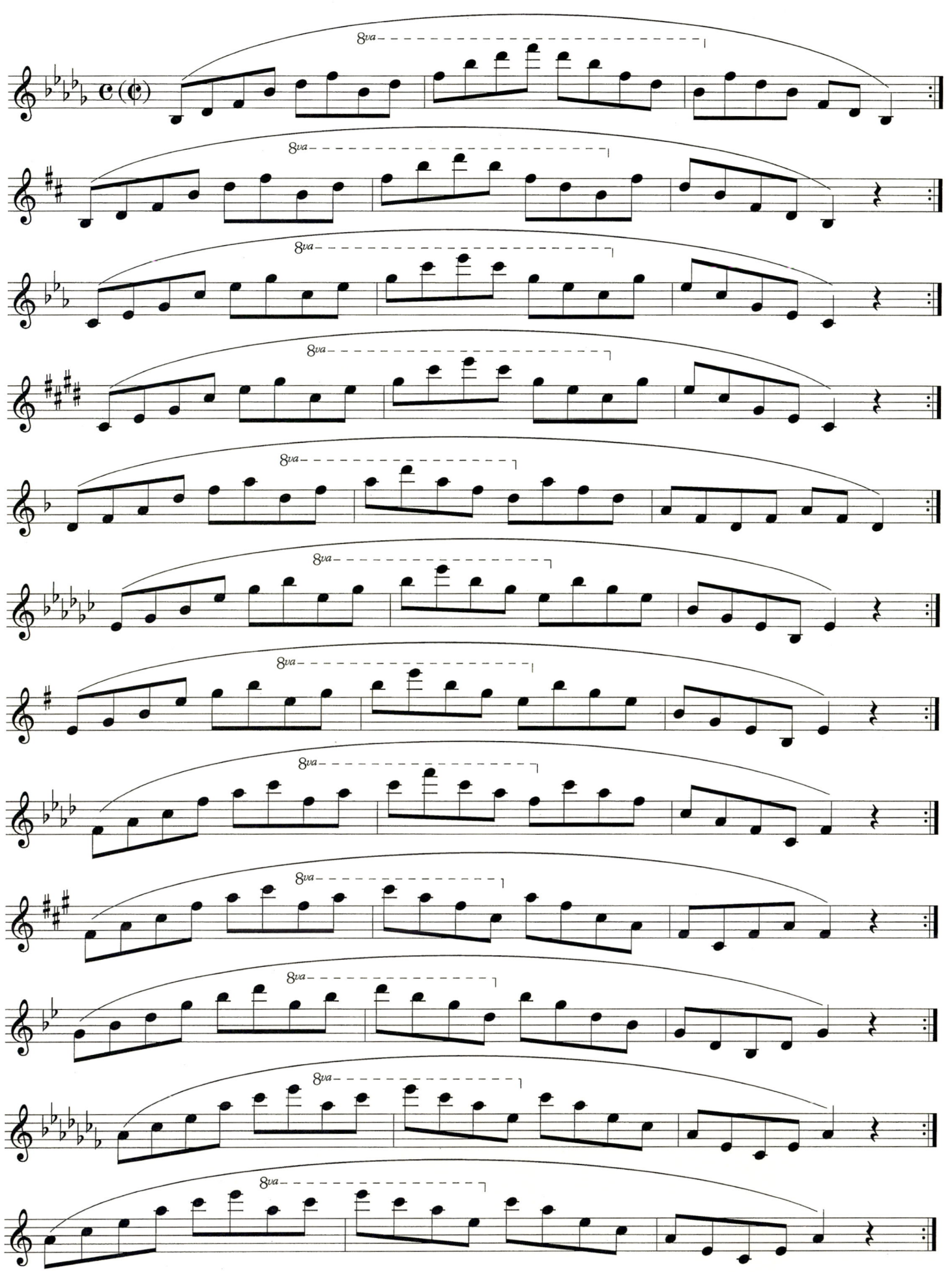

Minor Scales, Melodic: One Octave
Use as many combinations of modes as possible.

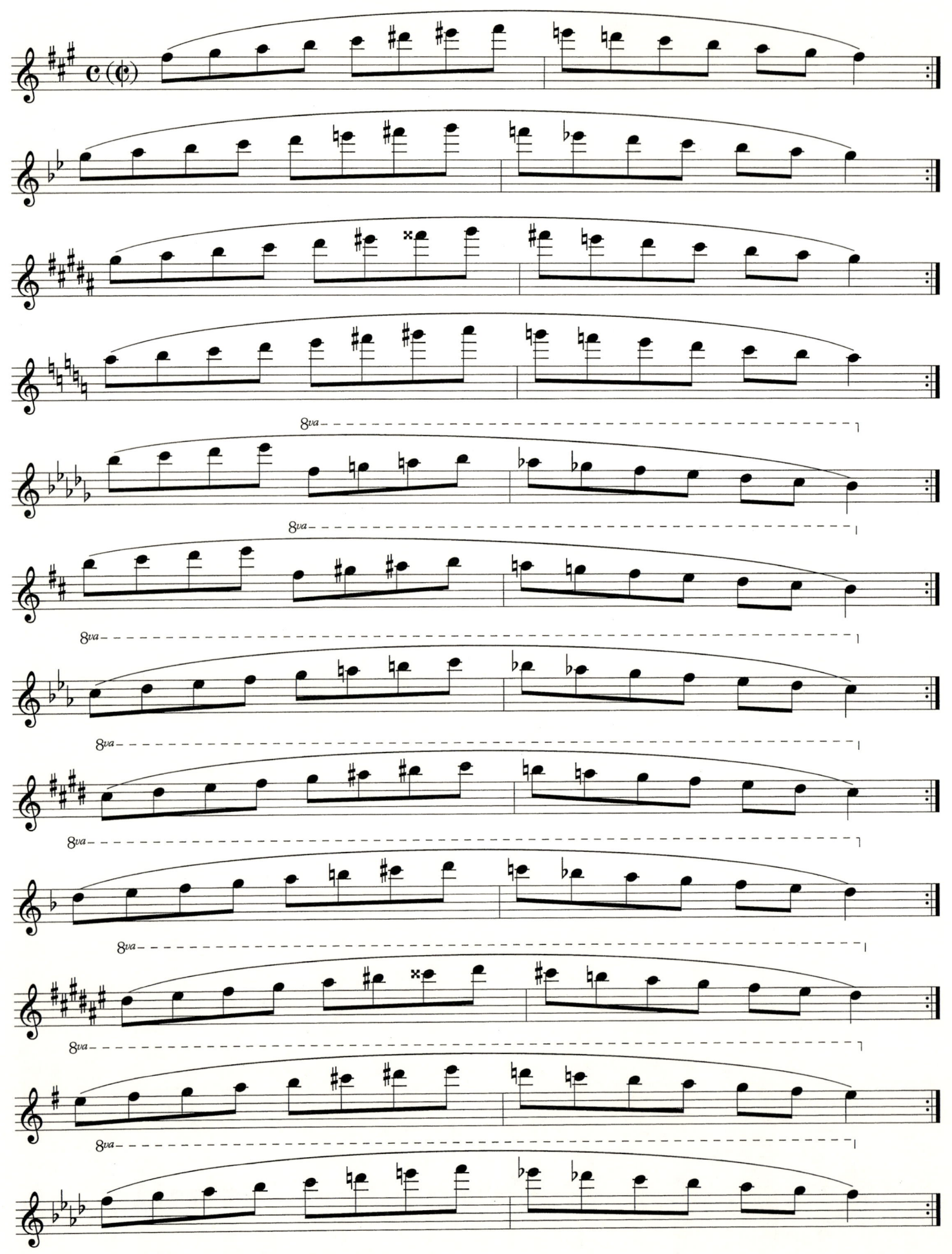

Minor Scales, Melodic: Extended Range
Use as many combinations of modes as possible.

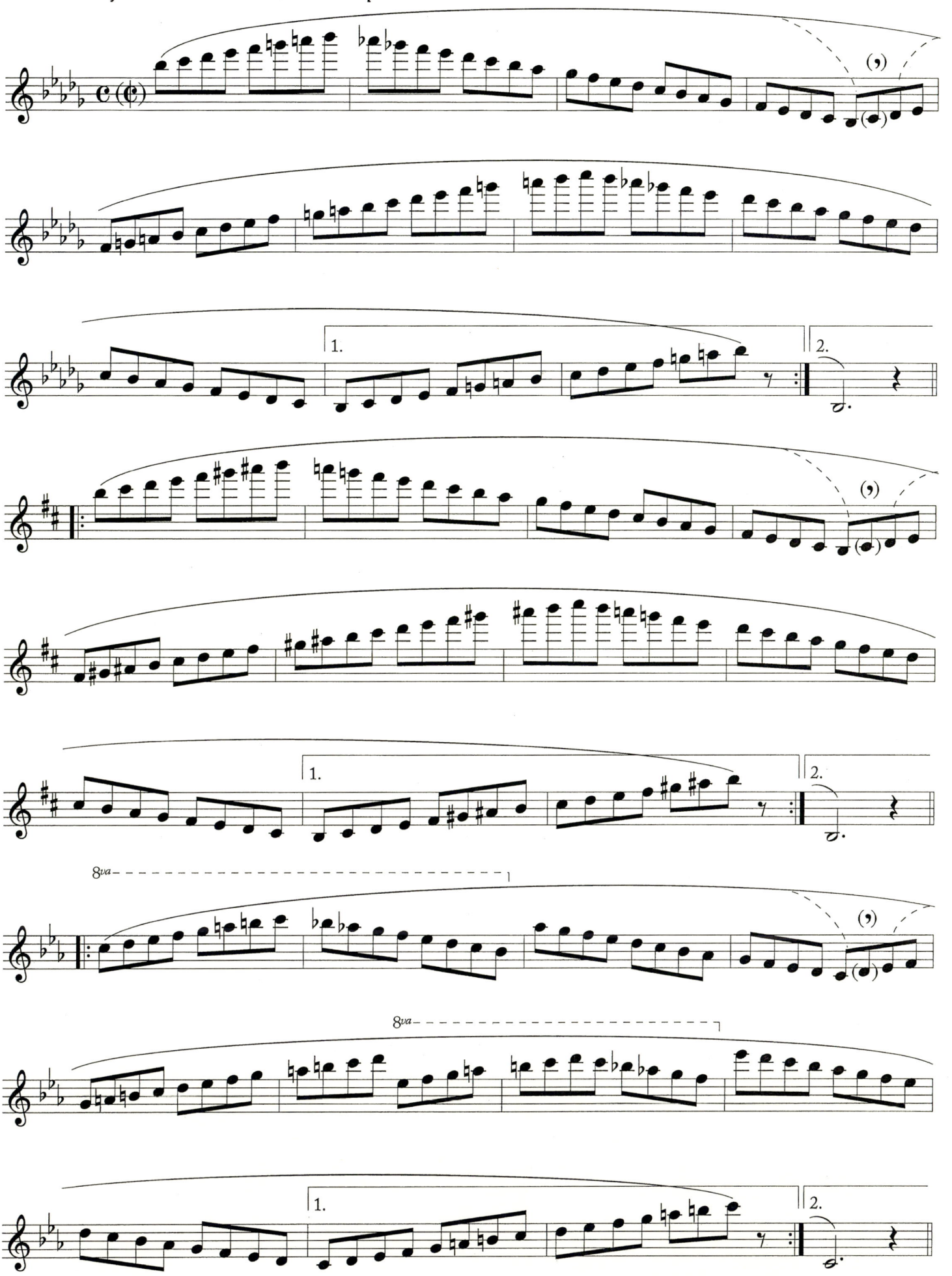

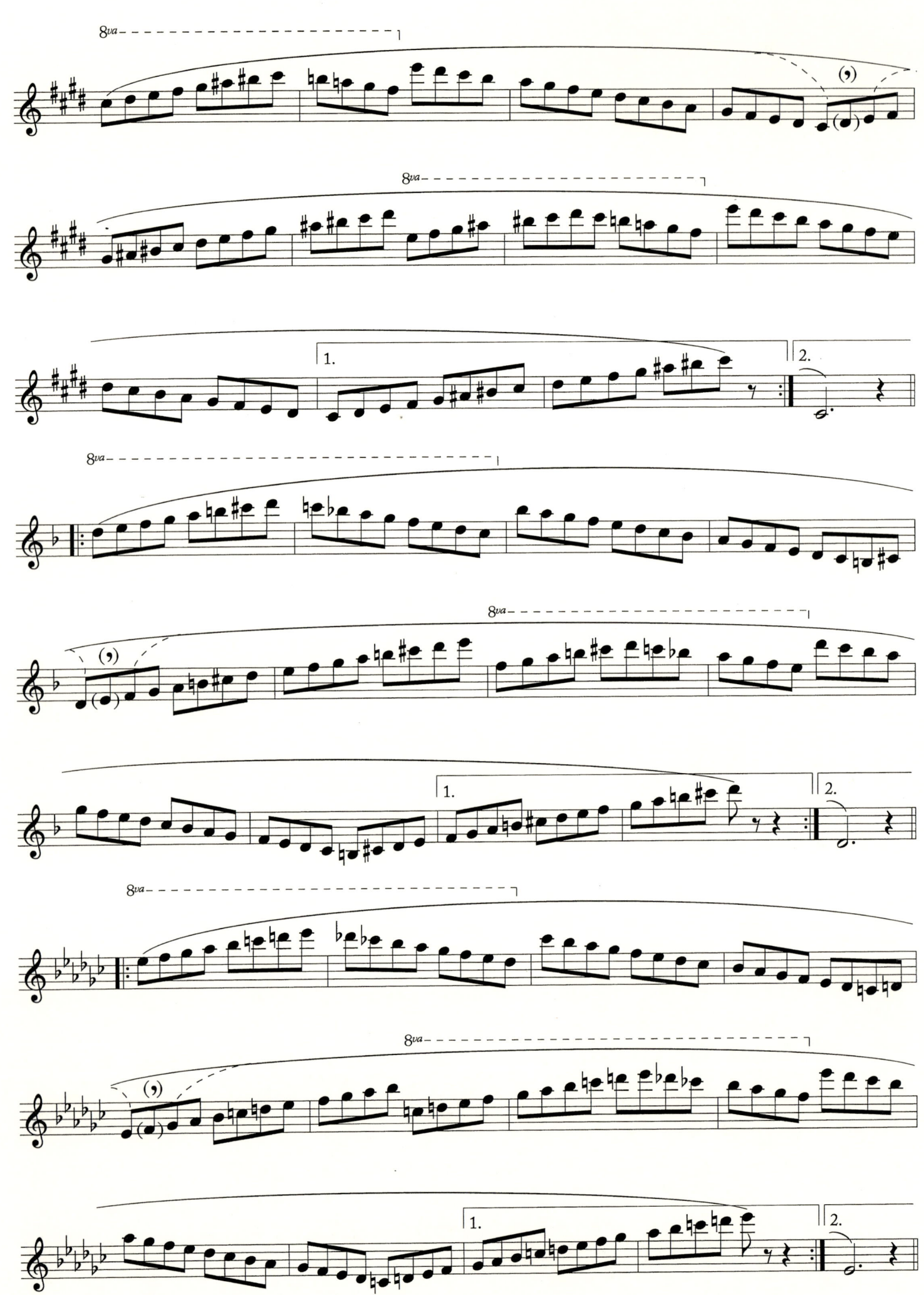

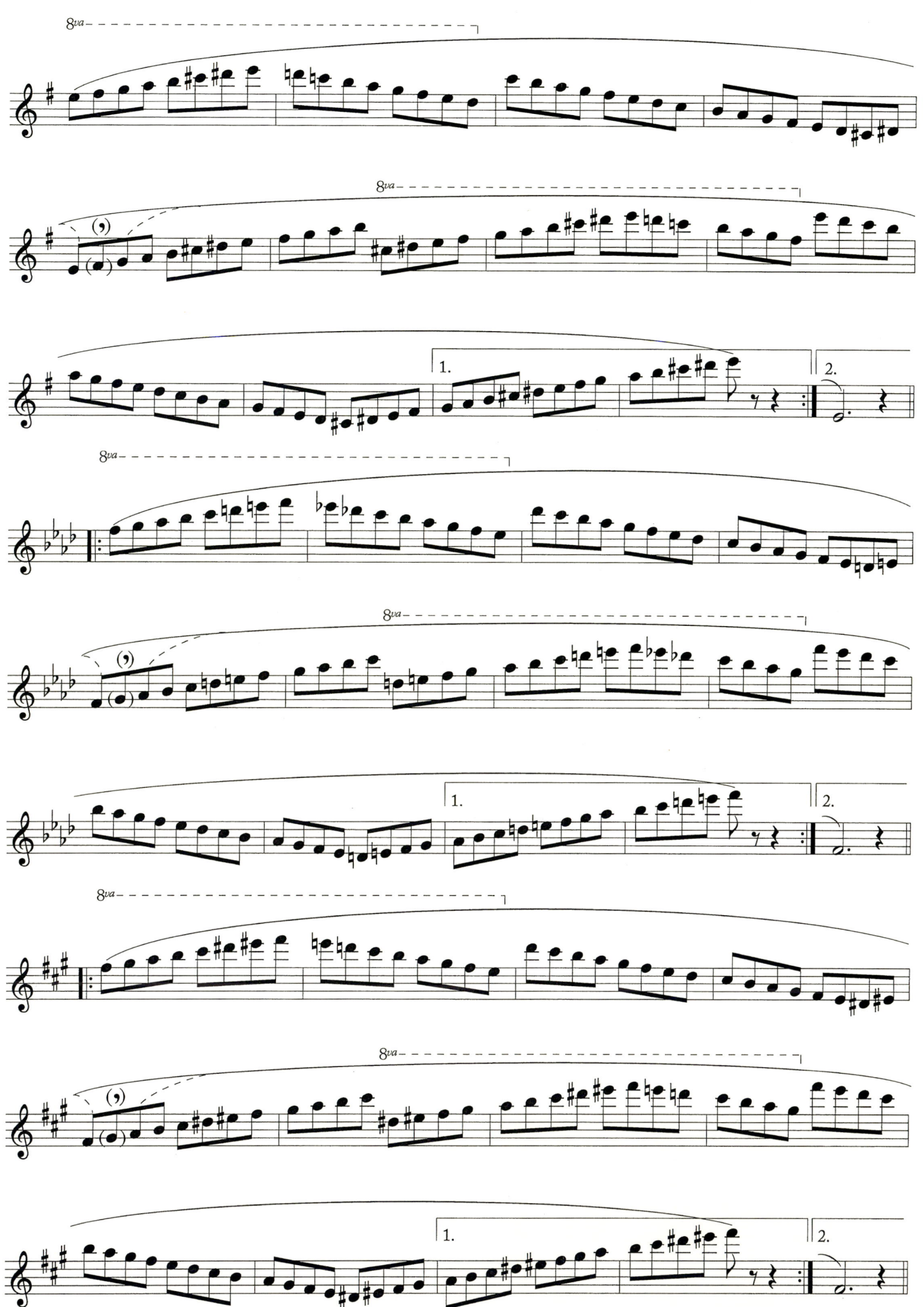

Whole-tone Scales
Use as many combinations of modes as possible.

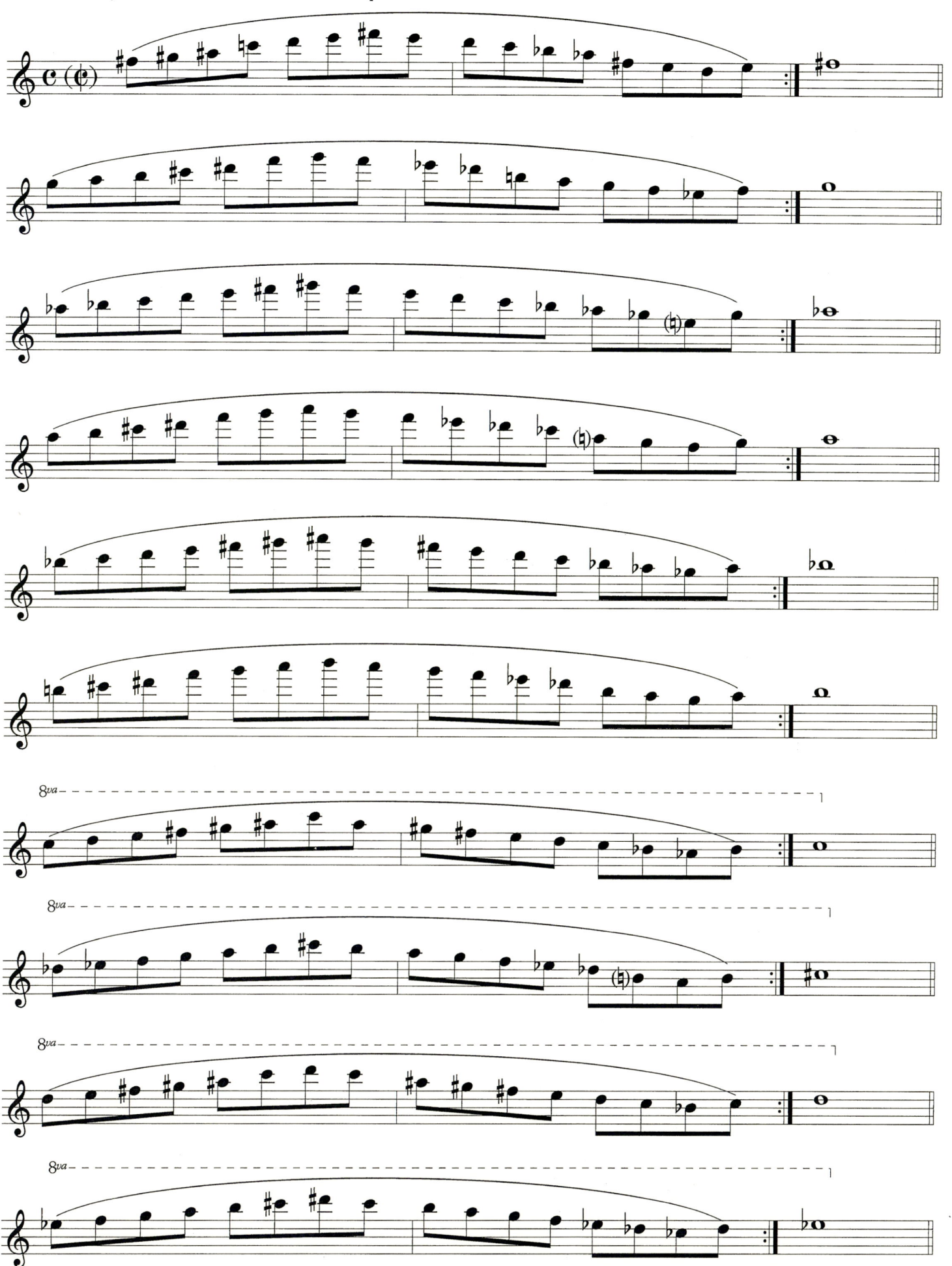

Diminished (Octatonic) Scales
Use as many combinations of modes as possible.

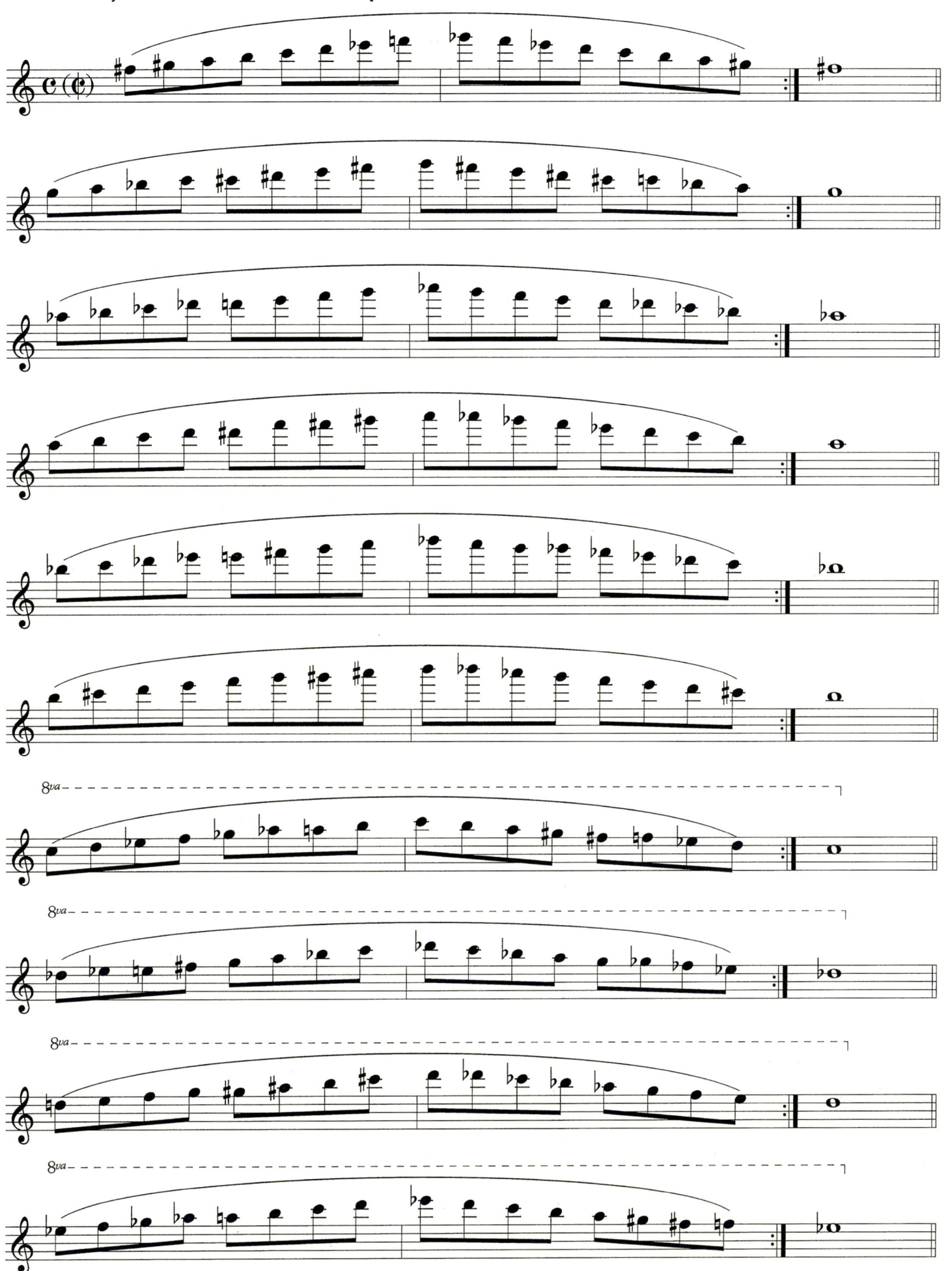

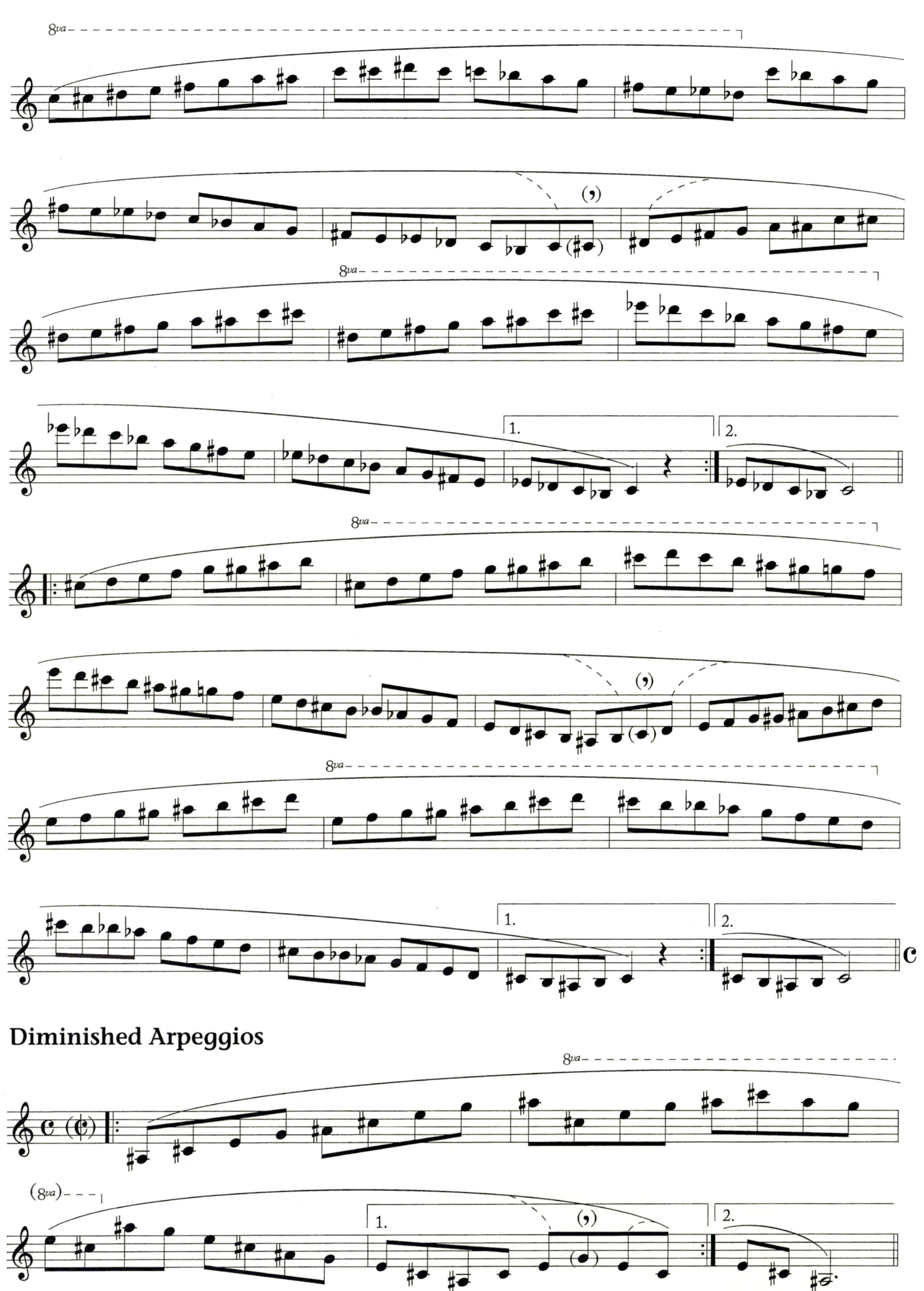

Diminished Arpeggios

Patterns in Thirds

Use as many combinations of modes as possible.

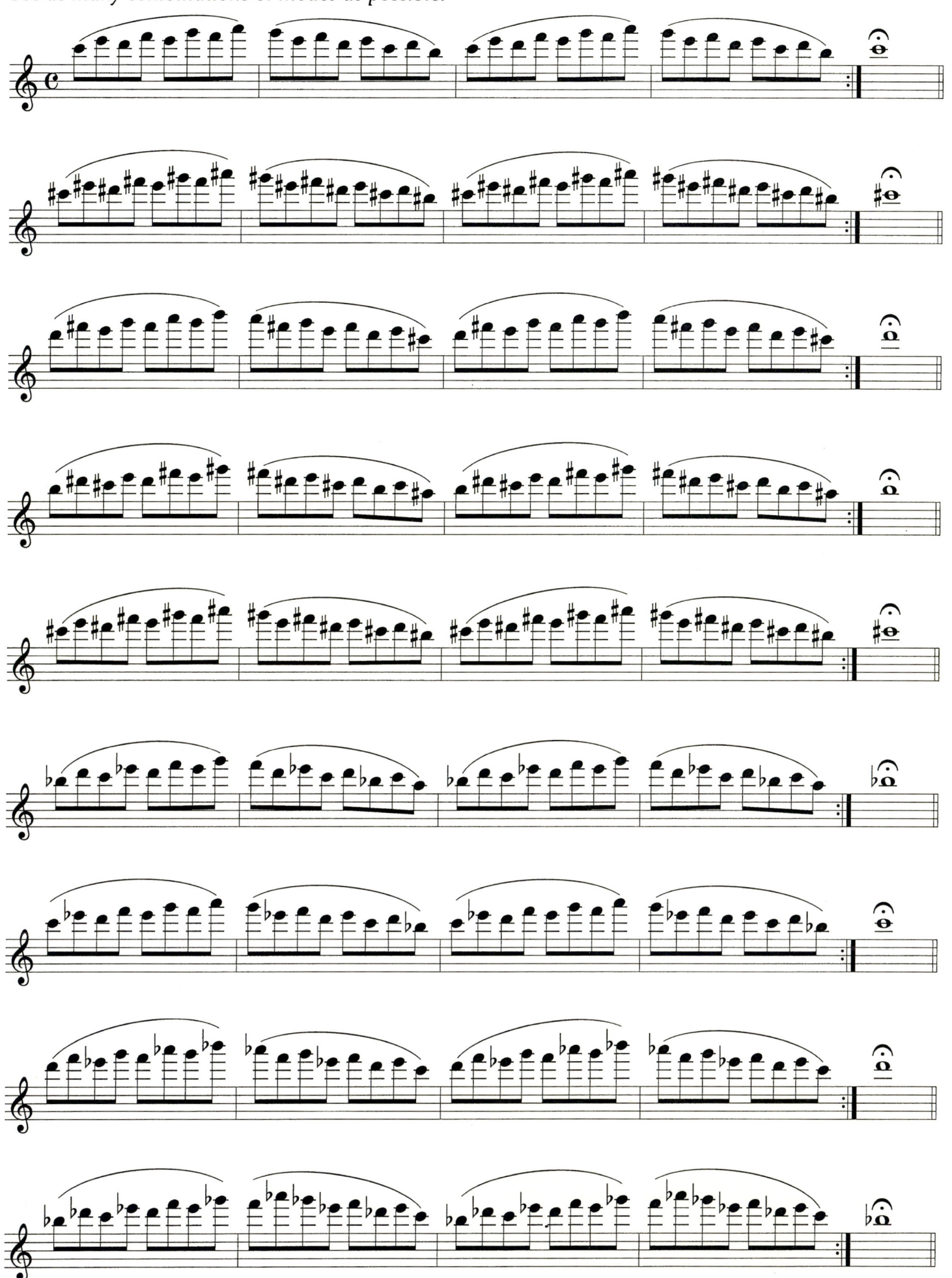

Pentatonic Scales
Use as many combinations of modes as possible.

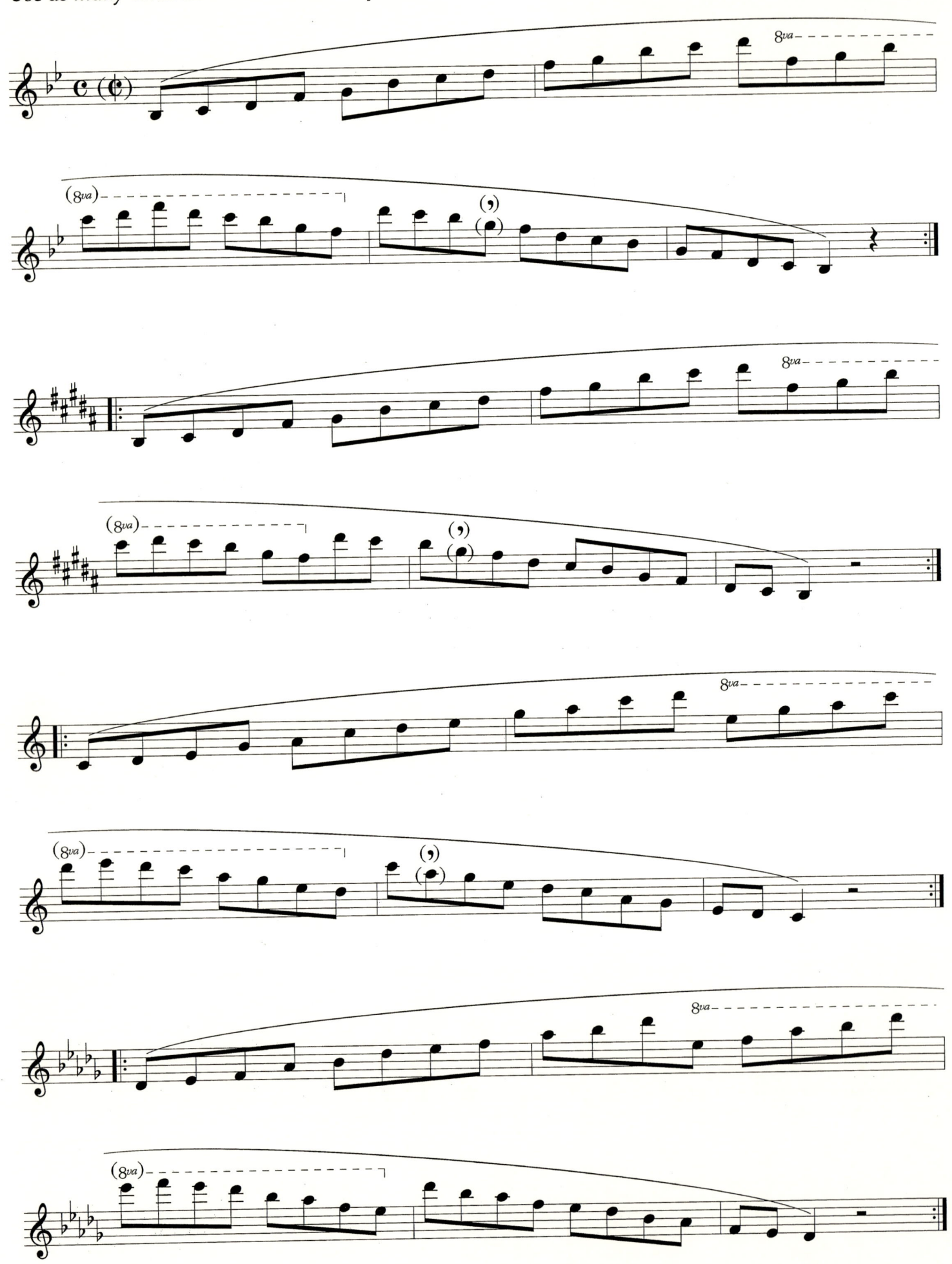

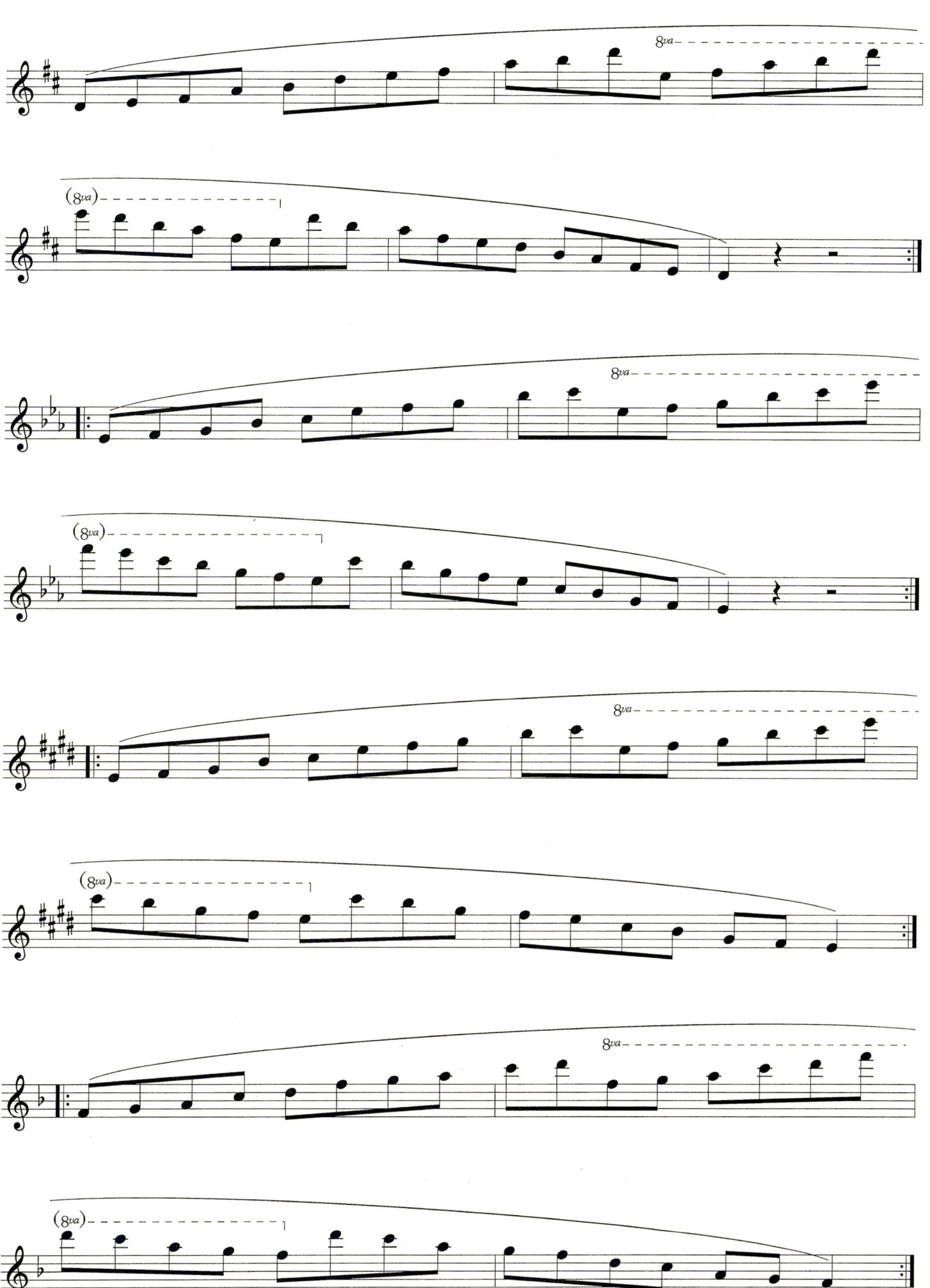

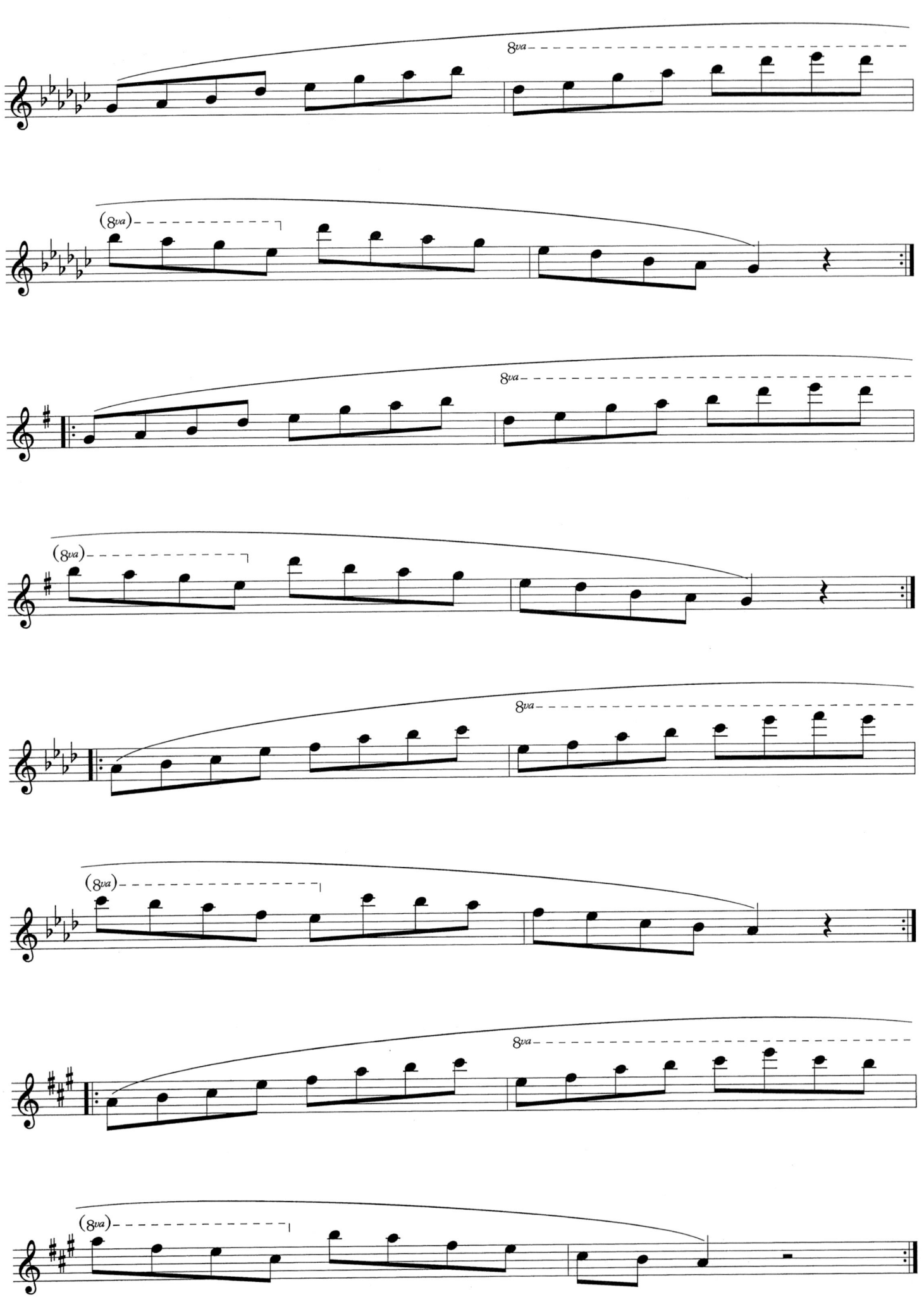

ARTICULATING THE HIGH TONES

When the above-normal tones are played, a proportionally smaller quantity of air is used as the frequency of vibration increases. In other words, as one plays higher the air stream becomes increasingly smaller.

This phenomenon accounts for the unusual feeling the performer experiences inside the mouth when first playing high tones. It has often been described as an "open throat", an unfortunate term for more than one reason. In the first place, ambiguity often takes place in the mind of a saxophonist, or any wind player for that matter, who is told for the first time to keep an "open throat." What is being referred to is the inside of the mouth and throat and its shape while playing, although it is impossible to see any of these shapes and functions! The consideration of tongue position, throat opening, etc.—must be translated into language that will produce a meaningful result.

Secondly, even fluoroscopic studies disprove the notion that the throat must be open in order to have the finer air stream required to emit the high tones successfully. Thus, the concept of mouthpiece pitches (see p. 1) is virtually indispensable since the player can relate the feeling of embouchure and air to a real pitch level on the unattached mouthpiece alone.

The tongue position and throat opening *do* change as one proceeds into the above-normal saxophone range. Because of this, the tongue is not in a position ordinarily used when tonguing tones in the saxophone's normal range. Therefore, the player who is first attempting the high tones will instinctively use the tonguing technique known to him by the countless hours of conditioning he has experienced. The result is almost invariably that no high tones will respond. This is why many of the examples and exercises in this book bear instructions *begin each tone without tonguing.*

Inasmuch as the tongue position is different for producing the high tones, it will also be different for articulating them. The following guidelines for tonguing in the above-normal range will be helpful.

1. Produce the desired tone without tonguing it.
2. Repeat the above until the tone is started clearly.
3. Start the tone again by tonguing it.
4. Practice starting the tone, alternating it by tonguing and not tonguing.
5. The tongue, while used for articulation, must remain as near as possible to the position necessary for high-tone production.
6. Repeat the above, working toward the goal of increasing the speed of articulation in the high-tone range.

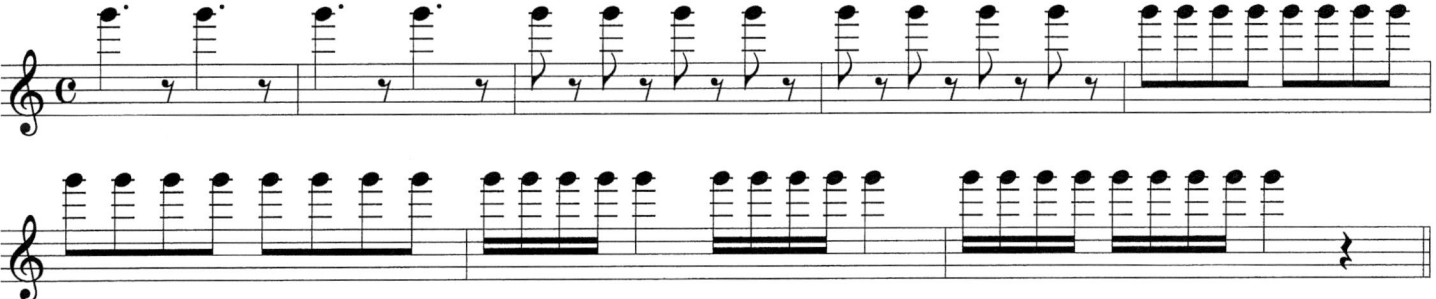

At this point, any and all of the preceding pages of studies may be repeated using various articulations.

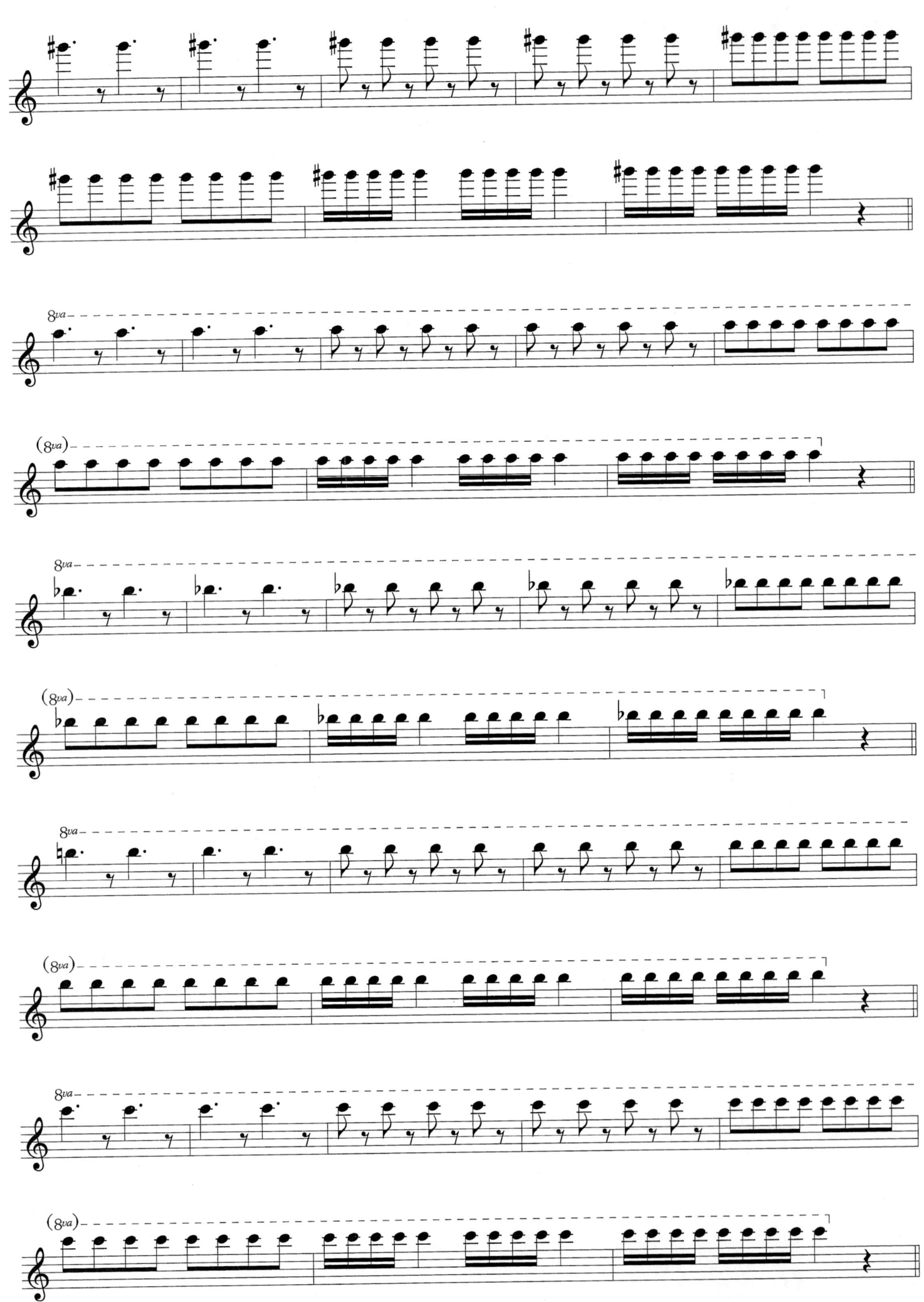

80

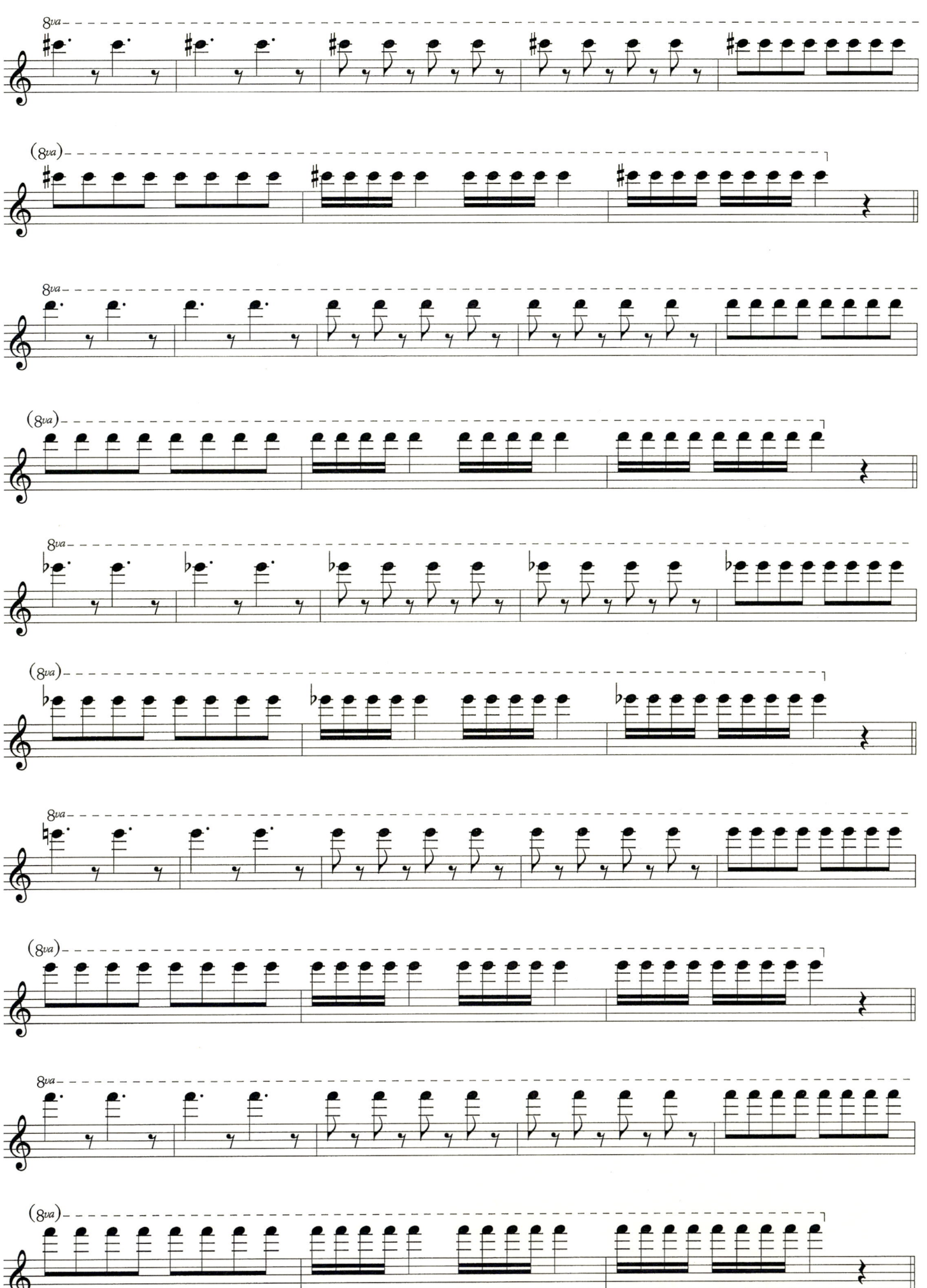

Eugene Rousseau has established himself as one of the leading saxophone performers and pedagogues in the world today. Currently a member of the artist faculty of the School of Music at the University of Minnesota, he is Distinguished Professor Emeritus of Music at the Indiana University Jacobs School of Music. His many students have distinguished themselves as university professors and superb performers throughout the world. He has received prestigious guest professor appointments at the Paris Conservatory, the Hochschule für Musik of Vienna, Arizona State, and the Universities of Iowa, Nebraska, and North Texas. Eugene Rousseau has appeared as soloist with numerous orchestras throughout the world, including the Minnesota, Indianapolis Symphony, BBC, Bavarian Radio, Prague Symphony, Kansai Philharmonic, and Austrian Radio orchestras. His performances have been heard on NPR's *Performance Today*, *Adventures in Good Music*, and has been interviewed on *Morning Edition*.

In 1969 Rousseau co-founded the World Saxophone Congress, the first such organization for an individual instrument, considered by many to be a major turning point in establishing credibility for the saxophone as a serious medium of musical expression. The North American Saxophone Alliance honored him with its highest award – Honorary Life Membership. Eugene Rousseau attended the Chicago Musical College, Northwestern University, and earned the Ph.D. in Music Literature and Peformance at the University of Iowa, where his principal teacher was Dr. Himie Voxman. In 1960 Rousseau was awarded a Fulbright Grant to study the saxophone with Marcel Mule at the Paris Conservatory. During this time Rousseau also had the opportunity to study wind acoustics with the eminent Charles Houvenaghel. In 1964, he was appointed to the faculty of the School of Music at Indiana University, where he taught for 36 years. While at Indiana, he was for twenty years the chief consultant for saxophone research and development for the Yamaha Corporation of Japan.